HOUSE PLANTS

ANTONY MASON

HOUSE PLANTS

With the compliments of
Ariel

**GEDDES &
GROSSET**

First published in 1988 by
  Geddes & Grosset Ltd
  New Lanark Mills
  Lanark
  Scotland
  ML11 9DB

Designed and typeset by Catchword Editorial Services

Line drawings by Antony Mason

Colour illustrations by Davis Meltzer and reproduced by
kind permission of Time-Life Books.
© 1972 Time-Life Books Inc.

© 1988 Geddes & Grosset Ltd

Printed in Great Britain by
Richard Clay (The Chaucer Press) Ltd,
Bungay, Suffolk

Contents

ACKNOWLEDGEMENT

The author owes a great debt of thanks to
Peter Jones, of Manningford Bruce Nurseries,
for his much valued opinions and expert
advice in the preparation of this book.

Introduction

House plants have been with us since ancient times. We might not go as far as suggesting that they are essential to human existence, but clearly they do fulfil a need: perhaps it has something to do with the way in which we enclose ourselves in architecture, fostering within us a deep yearning for the reassuring presence of nature. House plants may only be a token gesture in response to this, but it is none the less one that receives devoted attention from all those – professionals and non-professionals alike – who take an interest in the appearance of the places we live in. How desolate, we all think, a building looks without any greenery to set off the hard edge of the masonry; and how dry and inhospitable a living room, no matter how exquisitely furnished, without some kind of house plants.

It is probably no coincidence that the great boom in interest in house plants during the Victorian era coincided with rapid industrialization and the massive expansion of the towns. Plant hunters, sometimes facing extraordinary hardships, trod the world in search of species that could be nurtured in the glasshouses of the wealthy and the smoke-filled, gas-lit parlours of the less well-to-do. House plants were in vogue, and the thirst for them was insatiable. We have inherited much of this tradition, not only in the way that we treat house plants as decoration, but also in that many of our house plants today are descendants or relatives – often carefully adapted or hybridized by the professional growers – of these highly-prized Victorian specimens.

It was not of course simply the fascination for exotic things that had the plant hunters searching the tropical

forests of South America or the mountains of western China
for suitable subjects. That played its part, but more
important were the demands of the environment in which
these new plants were to be grown. If a home presented the
same climate as the garden outside, we could decorate it
with plants brought in from the garden: but in fact a home
presents a quite different picture. By and large our houses
are shady and dry; the temperatures are likely to fluctuate
wildly, especially in winter when heating systems might
roast a room at 75°F (24°C) during the day and evening, and
then allow the temperature to drop to just above freezing in
the middle of the night. These are not conditions that plants
take kindly to. The wide variety of house plants, however,
ensures that, no matter what conditions prevail in the
house, there is almost always a plant that will survive. We
have to accept, too, that certain plants will never do very
well in the home, but have attractive features, such as
superb flowers, that entice us to keep them as best we can
until we have to discard them.

No plant, however, is happy in conditions that do not
favour it, and not even the toughest plant can withstand
endless neglect. To keep house plants well and looking at
their best, you have to know the requirements of each one
individually. Some thrive in a warm, humid atmosphere
where others collapse and rot at the mere suggestion of it;
some hate being too heavily watered, others (the precious
few) can never be given too much water; some need plenty
of sunlight and others scorch in it. One of the ways to think
about what each house plant needs is to cast your mind back
to those plant hunters and consider in what kind of
conditions they would have found the plant growing in its
natural state: the tropical rainforests of South America are
warm and humid; most of China and Japan is temperate, as
is the Mediterranean region; the desert receives masses of
sunlight and only intermittent rain. Conditions presented

to a plant imported into the home from afar should reflect these origins to some degree at least.

Looking after house plants does require some thought and effort: there is no escaping it. If you have a range of plants, you cannot simply water the whole lot on a day each week and you cannot expect them to grow equally well wherever you put them. The trouble is, however, that most of us really do not have the time or inclination to plan out a carefully staggered programme of watering and feeding. And most of us have homes that have perhaps only one or two windowsills that receive good light, and then they may be directly over a radiator producing fatal quantities of heat. We can only do the best that we can.

Some people claim that if you talk to your plants comfortingly every day they will grow better: you may not wish to go quite that far, but there is no doubt that if you do pay some attention to your plants regularly you will learn their needs and be able to spot the first signs of distress if the conditions that you have provided are in some way unsuitable.

Position and temperature

Each plant has its own preferred amount of light. For most house plants this is bright indirect light, so a windowsill that receives no direct sunlight, or only very little, is ideal. Although some plants will tolerate extremely shady conditions quite happily, some light is essential, for without light photosynthesis cannot take place. This is the process whereby magnesium-based pigments called chlorophylls in the plant's leaves absorb the energy provided by light, which is then used by the plant to convert carbon-dioxide and water into the carbohydrates – such as starch and sugar – which it needs in order to grow. Chlorophylls are green, which is why leaves are green. This explains why the plants that can survive in the shade tend to have dark-green leaves, indicating that these leaves have a greater concentration of chlorophyll and so can make better use of the limited light. It also explains why variegated plants, which have green leaves splashed or striped with white or cream coloration, need more light, because they have less chlorophyll.

Strong artificial lighting can take the place of natural light, but the daily dose of artificial light should be rather greater than ordinary daylight. This may not be practical in the home, but of course it can make sense in offices and studios where strong lighting is on all day.

Standard room temperature is acceptable for most house plants, but again each has its individual preferences. Very few will survive frost, or near-freezing temperatures. Plants placed on a windowsill may need to be protected from the low temperatures that can occur immediately next to the glass in winter; before drawing the curtains at night, remove the plants from the windowsills. Similarly, the sun streaming through glass in summer can cause scorching.

If a plant looks unhappy and starts dropping its leaves in conditions which otherwise seem perfect, this may be due to overwatering, but could also be caused by a draught. The plant may well revive simply by being moved to another, draught-free position.

Watering

Strangely, the most common threat to house plants is not so much neglect as overwatering. All plants need moisture in some form or other, and in varying quantities. Water, and the essential minerals dissolved in it, is usually taken up by the roots of the plant. But these roots must also have some air: the process whereby the water drains through soil also pulls in air, but if the soil is waterlogged, the roots become swamped and cannot function.

As a rule it is best to water plants thoroughly as occasion demands, removing the excess water that drains through the soil, and then leaving them until the next thorough watering. Providing water in little dribs and drabs on an irregular basis does little to meet the plant's changing needs as the year progresses.

It is important to observe these changing needs. In general you should water considerably more in summer than in winter. This is partly because in summer the plant is likely to be growing and using up more energy; but it is also because during warm weather moisture will evaporate from the plant's leaves and, in order to replace this lost moisture, the plant will draw more moisture up from the roots, a process called transpiration.

Many plants, such as Azaleas, take great dislike to water containing lime. This presents a difficulty to anyone living in a hard-water area. Filtering water will remove the lime, but also all the beneficial minerals. The best solution is to use nature's lime-filter: the sky. Rainwater is soft, and ideal for watering, or spraying, all house plants, and with a little forethought it is not difficult to collect it in sufficient quantities.

Humidity

The dryness of our houses provides one quality which most plants detest – especially those that originate from the steamy atmosphere of the tropical rainforests. There are two solutions: evaporation or aerial-spraying.

Because water naturally vaporizes at room temperature, it is possible to provide a continual supply of moist air to a plant by keeping the area around its base damp. The easiest way to do this is to stand the pot on a flat tray of gravel which is kept constantly wet; the stones, however, should be large enough so the pot does not actually sit in the water.

Another method is to pack the plant pot into an outer container filled with peat or sand or moss which is kept permanently moist. By such means, you create a little damp environment (or 'microclimate') around the plant, just humid enough to counteract the damaging dryness of the surrounding air.

Aerial-spraying is a more direct method of providing humidity. It involves, quite simply, spraying the plant with a fine mist of water (rainwater, for preference). Plastic spray-bottles, with fine nozzles, are widely available and not expensive. You may feel, however, that your furniture and curtains will not benefit from aerial-spraying; if you cannot move the plant to spray it you will have to decide on your priorities.

Plant foods

The soil or compost in which a house plant grows contains a large quantity of minerals and nutrients, but in time, especially if it is growing strongly, the plant will probably have used up most of these nutrients and they will need replenishment.

House plant foods can be bought at any garden shop and even in supermarkets, usually in the form of a liquid solution to be mixed with water and supplied at the same time as you water the plants. These plant foods usually contain nitrogen, phosphorus and potassium, the three elements vital to healthy plant growth.

It is simple really: all you have to do is to mix up the plant food according to the instructions and feed your plants according to their requirements. Most plants will not require any feeding at all if they are young or have been recently repotted: wait six months before commencing feeding. And most established plants will only require feeding from spring to autumn, and should not be fed over winter; however, winter-flowering plants may need feeding over winter. Do not, by the way, think you are doing your plant a favour by mixing a stronger dose of plant food than is recommended on the label: this is liable to harm the plant or cause ungainly growth.

The hard-pressed or forgetful house-plant owner may like to take advantage of the plant food that comes in 'slow-release' granules, which provide a steady supply of nutrients over a period of four months or so. This is a useful convenience, but of course cannot take the place of more sensitive judgements of a plant's requirements.

Propagation

As with all forms of life, one of the essential roles of plants is to create another generation, thereby ensuring the contin-uation of the species. Many house plants perform this function with remarkable ease, and it is not usually difficult to create new plants from those you already have. Several methods of propagation are possible: the selection of the appropriate one will depend on the plant in question.

Some plants make the job of propagation extremely easy by producing ready-made **plantlets**. The Spider Plant (*Chlorophytum*) is a well-known example of this, producing young plantlets at the end of long shoots: these will root themselves without any help from you, given half the chance. Other plants, especially the Bromeliads, produce **offsets**, young plants that grow at the base of the mother plant and which can, when big enough, be separated off and potted on their own.

Cuttings provide another important means of propaga-tion. Stem-tip cuttings are made from the growing shoots, clipped off below one or two leaves, dipped in a rooting-compound (either a powder or a liquid), which contains hormones to encourage roots to develop, and planted in

moist soil. Alternatively, roots can be encouraged to grow
before planting by standing the cutting in plain water. Stem
cuttings involve a similar process, except here a middle
section of stem – sometimes, but not always, including a
leaf – is encouraged to root and to sprout shoots. Propagation from leaf cuttings is perhaps the most remarkable of
all: by taking a leaf of certain plants (such as the African
Violet, *Saintpaulia*), slashing its veins and then pinning it to
moist soil, tiny plantlets will appear on the leaf where the
veins have been cut through. With many plants propagation by cuttings is only really feasible when you can provide
constant warmth and humidity, for which a specially
designed, perspex-topped cabinet called a propagator is the
best answer. However, by covering a pot with a plastic bag
and keeping this in a warm place you could be in with a
chance. Whether using a propagator or a plastic bag,
remember to lift the cover every day for five minutes in
order to prevent the humidity from inducing rot.

Many plants can be propagated by **division**, which
simply means that you divide the roots – or in some cases
the bulb-like tuber – into sections, each with growing
shoots attached, and repot these.

Air-layering is a rather specialized form of propagation
that only applies to certain plants, such as the Rubber
Plant, *Ficus elastica*. An incision is made with a sharp knife
in the stem below a growing point and some leaves; this is
held open with a piece of matchstick or a pebble and dabbed
with rooting compound. Damp moss is then bound around
the incision and a sheet of polythene is sealed over the moss.
Roots will begin to grow into the moss and when sufficiently developed the whole of the growing tip, with its new
roots, can be cut away from the main plant and repotted.

Lastly, some house plants can be readily grown from
seed. This applies particularly to plants from temperate
climates, such as Cyclamen and Busy Lizzie (*Impatiens*).

Soil

The soil that you use for your house plants becomes important when it comes to repotting or propagation. The exact nature of the perfect soil for each plant is a precise art best left to the expert. In the meantime we can take advantage of the commercially produced soil and peat-based potting composts. Ordinary garden soil, by the way, is not appropriate: it has neither the richness nor the texture suitable for house plants, but what it might well have is pests, weeds and diseases.

The packaged composts are either loam-based or peat-based. Loam is a prepared soil that is rich in decomposed organic material; this is combined with peat, sand and a standard mix of base fertilizer. No. 1 contains less base fertilizer and so is more suitable for young plants; No. 2 and No. 3 are usually the ones to use for repotting established plants. Peat-based composts are similar, except that they do not contain soil, and so are rather lighter and more airy, thus fostering different kinds of root structure.

Repotting becomes necessary when a plant becomes 'pot-bound': this occurs when the roots have grown too big for the pot. It is easily enough recognized: roots will appear through the holes in the base of the pot, or, if the pot is removed, they can be seen lining the edge of the soil in a thick mat, desperately looking for somewhere to go. If you do not repot a pot-bound plant its growth will be restricted and may even become distorted. Most plants are best repotted in spring, ready for the new season's growth.

Plants need soil for two reasons: first, as a source of nutrients, and second to provide stability. Ways have been devised of doing away with soil completely. All the nutrients that a plant requires can be supplied in specially prepared measures dissolved in water. For stability, the plant's roots can be held firm by large granules of porous clay. This technique, known as 'hydroculture', works well with certain kinds of common house plants and is useful to offices and institutions where there is no one to give daily attendance to the plants. But its modern technology has not yet been able to supplant soil completely, for it would seem that soil is a more reliable medium in which to play out the delicate balances between plants and their nutrients; thus hydroculture has not yet caught on in the world of house plants to the extent that was at one time predicted.

Pests and diseases

One of the drawbacks about bringing a bit of nature into the home is that one is never sure quite how much uninvited nature comes with it. House plants are prone to pests and diseases: there is nothing unusual about this, and most ills are curable, but if ignored for too long the plant, as well as others near it, may be irreparably damaged.

There are five common pests. All of them feed off the plants and will gradually cause stunted growth or yellowing leaves. Three of them create an additional nuisance by depositing a sticky gunge called 'honeydew' around the plant; these are: aphids (usually greenfly); whitefly, the larvae of which feed off the leaves; and scale insects, which are like tiny scabs on the underside of the leaves, green when young, but turning brown with age. The other two common pests are red spider mites, miniscule insects (not actually spiders at all) which display the distinctive signs of their occupation by the presence of fine webs on the underside of the leaves; and mealy bugs, which congregate into groups like blobs of fluffy cotton wool.

All of these pests can be destroyed by using a standard insecticide spray for house plants, which will be based on derris, pyrethrum or permethrin, or a similar effective chemical. However, do be very careful with sprays: read the instructions and take all the precautions they recommend. In fact spraying with insecticide should really only be a last resort: small infestations can usually be picked off by hand, or sponged away, or even washed away by immersing the plant in tepid water with a touch of liquid soap added to it. Scale insects and mealy bugs can be removed by wiping them over with cotton wool dipped in methylated spirits.

Rot and mildew are only likely to occur on certain plants that are prone to them, such as Flowering Begonias. In the case of rot, the cause will almost always be overwatering: it may destroy the plant completely, but you can try saving it by removing all the damaged parts and treating the affected region with powdered sulphur or a spray containing fungicide. Mildew is rather less dramatic, but still needs to be stamped out in its early stages by applying sulphur or fungicides to the affected leaves.

Plant training

It is only too easy to become attached to an old and straggly house plant that has outlived its original attractions. What purpose this sentimentality serves is anyone's guess: certainly unsightly plants do little justice to their cause, for their purpose, surely, is to bring the freshness, vitality and beauty of nature into our homes.

To rear house plants effectively a certain amount of ruthlessness is required: by pruning a plant back hard you will force it to divert its energies into new growth; by pinching out growing tips that threaten to make the plant leggy, you will encourage side shoots and make it more bushy; and by chucking out plants that are past their best and beyond recall you will be making room for new plants, perhaps even ones you have propagated yourself. There are, after all, hundreds of other house plants to choose from, each bringing its own rewards and merits.

An A–Z of house plants

The following list of house plants tells you what you need to know to keep you plants happy and healthy. There are over sixty plants listed here, chosen because they are the ones you are most likely to come across in the shops, or be presented with as a gift. Inevitably there will be omissions, given the vast numbers of house plants on the market and the fact that, with the renewed interest in house plants generally, new plants, varieties and hybrids are being introduced all the time.

The alphabetical order of the plants in this A–Z is by Latin name. Confusing, you may think, but the names of our house plants *are* confusing. Take the *Tradescantia fluminensis*, for example: widely known as Wandering Jew, it also known as Wandering Sailor, Spiderwort, and Inch Plant. It would be misleading to give preference to any of these common names, so we must rely on the Latin name, daunting though it may seem, in order to apply a scheme that we can agree on.

Unfortunately not everyone agrees on the Latin names either. Many of our plants have two alternative names and it seems to be a matter of personal preference which is used: the Paradise Palm or Kentia Palm, for example, is referred to as *Howea forsteriana* in some books, and as *Kentia forsteriana* in others. Some plants belonging to closely related groups seem to have names that are used more or less interchangeably: Marantas and Calatheas (the Prayer Plant family) are examples of this, even though, strictly speaking, there are botanical differences between them. Wherever there is a common confusion of names, both names are given in this A–Z, and the index should help you find the plant you are looking for if it is not listed in the A–Z under the name that you expect.

All plants are divided into families, which share certain botanical characteristics. A large number of house plants, for instance, belong to the aroid or Arum family (Araceae, to give it its Latin name). The Latin names of individual plants begin with the genus, the group name for related plants within the family. The second name identifies the species itself, and the last name (if there is one) the particular subspecies, variety or hybrid. Thus one kind of Bromeliad is called *Neoregelia carolinae tricolor*: *Neoregelia* is the genus, *carolinae* is the species, and *tricolor* is the subspecies. One type of Hibiscus is called *Hibiscus* (genus) *rosa-sinensis* (species) 'Moonlight' (hybrid).

Adiantum capillus-veneris
'Maidenhair Fern'

This is surely one of the prettiest and most delightful of ferns, with a poetic name to match. This refers to the tiny, petal-like leaves that make up the fronds: they look like miniature forms of the leaves of the oriental gingko tree, known as the Maidenhair Tree, hence the shared name.

The leaves unfurl from delicate green stems that rise out of the soil, developing into arching fronds on wiry, brown stems up to 1 ft (30 cm) long and 5 in (13 cm) wide, creating a shower of fresh-looking greenery. More mature plants will show a ring of brown spores – the fern's equivalent of seeds – on the underside of the leaves.

The Maidenhair Fern has European ancestry and so is tolerant of our climate: however, it is not very tolerant of the dry conditions of our homes and one of the most frequent complaints about them is that the leaves dry out. Give this fern plenty of humidity, therefore. It will also need a fair amount of light, but not direct sunlight: a window that receives little direct sun is a good place, especially in a large kitchen or bathroom, where the humidity in the air is likely to be high.

These ferns are not too difficult to grow if you attend to their basic requirements. That said, they seem to be sensitive to the position they are given: for no good reason they can be happy in one place and quite miserable in

another, although the conditions in both places may be similar. So once you and the fern have agreed on the right spot, leave it there. If the fern is not doing well, cut back the dying fronds and try putting it somewhere else: these are resilient plants and recover well if they have been temporarily neglected.

There is a rather more robust version of the Maidenhair Fern, with bigger leaves and an altogether less dainty look, although still a pleasing plant: this is *Adiantum cuneatum*.

Adiantum capillus-veneris

Position: A fair amount of light, but not direct sunlight.
Temperature: Room temperature is fine; it will not like central-heating above 70°F (21°C) unless you give it plenty of humidity, and will not be happy at winter temperatures below 50°F (10°C).
Water: Keep moist throughout the year and do not allow the pot to dry out. As with most house plants, overwatering is the biggest threat: if left standing in water for any length of time, it will die. Supply the humidity essential to this plant by aerial-spraying, or by standing the pot on wet

gravel, or by setting the pot in an outer container packed with damp peat, sand or moss.

Feeding: Feed with a mild mix of plant food once a month during the summer months when the plant is growing.

Propagation: By division, breaking away a section of the fern with its roots and repotting; or by planting the spores in the spring (but this really needs a propagator).

Soil: Standard peat-based compost.

Problems: Leaves drying out: needs more water, or, more likely, more humidity. Leaves curling and sickly: too much water. Leaves pale: too much sunlight or needs feeding.

Aechmea fasciata

'Urn Plant' or 'Grecian Vase Plant'

This Bromeliad is one of the most spectacular house plants. Bromeliads (Bromeliaceae) form a huge family of some 1,400 species and, since they provide us with a number of characteristic house plants, we should begin with a word about Bromeliads in general.

Bromeliads are natives of tropical South America, where they are a common feature of the rainforests. They owe their family name to a seventeenth-century Swedish botanist, Olaf Bromel. Although some Bromeliads grow on the ground, many of them, including the Urn Plant, are what are known as epiphytes: they grow on other plants, usually trees. This is a quite benign relationship: they are not parasites, feeding off and harming their hosts as fungi do. The roots function simply as anchors, gripping tightly on to the bark of the tree. Whereas most plants use their roots to take water and nutrients from the soil, Bromeliads collect water in the central 'vase', a circular cavity from which the leaves radiate. In nature this can be the home of insects and even frogs, a little world of its own that supplies the Bromeliad with all the food it needs.

Bromeliads can produce spectacular flower-heads: these form in the central vase, sometimes staying low, sometimes – as in the case of the Urn Plant – rising high above the foliage on a long stem. These flower-heads will last for some time; but by and large, when the flowers fade, the Bromeliad will feel its life's work is done and will die.

However, it will by this time have produced one or more young plants from around its base (off-sets) which will go on to perform the same cycle.

The Urn Plant is an exuberant fountain of arching, strap-like leaves which spiral out from the central vase. These leaves are surprisingly thin, with the texture of parchment, and they are striped crossways by layers of

Aechmea fasciata

silvery dust; the thorny serrations along the edges of the leaves are quite sharp and can easily catch on to clothing.

The real interest of the Urn Plant is the flower-head, and this plant will usually be sold when it is already in flower. The flower-head looks something like a fir-cone or the leafy top of a pineapple, except that it is a radiant pink. The actual flowers themselves appear from the cavities between the bracts (modified leaves) of the flower-head and are a delicate purple and blue. The flower-heads last about four months, then wither.

Despite its exotic origins, the Urn Plant does not require any special treatment, as long as it has a fair amount of light and water. They are sometimes known by an alternative Latin name, *Billbergia rhodocyanea*.

Position: In sunlight or semi-shade: it is not fussy. However, you will need some room to show this plant off as it will grow to some 2 ft (60 cm) in overall width.

Temperature: Surprisingly tolerant. Avoid temperatures lower than 55°F (12°C), or very extreme heat.

Water: Keep the soil moist and always leave some water sitting in the central vase; use rainwater if your tapwater is hard.

Feeding: Once a month during the summer, mix a very mild solution of liquid fertilizer with the water to be poured into the central vase.

Propagation: After the original plant has flowered and died back, repot the young plants (offsets) that will have grown up around its base, preferably in spring

Soil: Use a lime-free, soil-less compost.

Problems: Rotting leaves: too much water in the soil, and probably too cold.

Aglaonema

'Chinese Evergreen'

The Chinese Evergreen is one of those delightful foliage house plants that exudes a happy freshness. In its ordinary form its has long, mid-green leaves which tumble forth on short stems. These days, however, you are much more likely to come across it in its variegated forms, which introduce cream or white into the leaf markings. One hybrid, the *Aglaonema trewbii* 'Silver Queen' has only small splashes of green on its silvery-white leaves.

As with the majority of variegated plants, the lighter the overall colour of the leaf-markings, the more light the plant will need, but none the less these plants will do well enough in poor light and are not troublesome to grow.

The Chinese Evergreen is one of the many house plants that comes from the Arum (or Araceae) family. Its proper home is in South East Asia. Although grown for its foliage, it may produce little white or yellow flowers during the summer, but this happy event may well pass unnoticed.

Position: Light or shade; even the variegated varieties are fairly tolerant.
Temperature: Standard room temperatures are fine, but in winter keep the room above 50°F (10°C).
Water: Water well in the summer, but keep drier over winter. To keep the plant healthy in hot temperatures, apply some humidity by aerial-spraying, or by placing the pot on a base of wet gravel.
Feeding: In summer, once a fortnight.
Propagation: From stem-tip cuttings; they will need warmth and humidity, preferably in a propagator. Or by root-division.
Soil: Standard potting compost.
Problems: If the plant is too cold, in a draught, or receives too much water it will begin to drop its leaves from the base; if not remedied, the plant will become straggly, with a scarred trunk. Prone to common pests, especially scale and mealy bug.

Anthurium scherzerianum
'Flamingo Flower' or 'Piggy Tail Plant'

The extraordinary flowers of this plant proved a fine test for those who have tried to stick a name to it. Flamingo Flower refers to the colour, usually a rather deeper red than flamingoes; Piggy Tail Plant refers to the gently curling flower-spike, or spadix; another common name, the Palette Plant, refers to the bright-red oval dish, the spathe, from which the spadix projects. There is a truth in all the names, but none quite captures the stunning impact of this plant's flowers.

The Anthuriums are further members of the Arum (or Araceae) family, cousins of, for example, the *Aglaonema*, the Chinese Evergreen. There is only one native British member of this family which, if somewhat less spectacular, shares some of the Anthuriums' characteristics: this is the *Arum maculatum*, the Lords-and-Ladies or Cuckoopint, with its cigar-like spadix sheltered by its pointed, light-green spathe.

Anthuriums come from tropical South America. The only species that is widely grown as a house plant is the *Anthurium scherzerianum*. Its flowers usually have a red spathe and spadix, but may also be pink or white. Another house-plant species is the *Anthurium andreanum*, the Oilcloth Plant, which has a creamy-white, waxy spadix set against a bright-red spathe, but this is harder to grow and really needs hothouse conditions. But even *Anthurium scherzerianum* is not exactly an easy customer: it is quite tricky to find the right balance of warmth and humidity that will allow it to flower from one year to the

Anthurium scherzerianum

next. Even so, all will not be entirely lost, for the foliage, with its elegant, tongue-like shapes and gently curving lines make an agreeable display. Alternatively, you can look upon these plants as temporary guests, to be discarded after flowering: they will, after all, last rather better than cut flowers.

Position: Plenty of light, but not direct sunlight.
Temperature: Warm: winter minimum of 60°F (16°C).
Water: Plenty of water in the summer; rather less in the winter. Humidity is important: in dry conditions spray daily with water; stand the pot on a base of wet gravel, or place the pot in an outer container packed with damp peat, sand or moss.
Feeding: Provide liquid plant food once a fortnight in the summer and when flowering.

Propagation: Divide the plant at the roots and repot.
Soil: Use a peat-based compost mixed with sphagnum moss and bark chippings, in equal quantities.
Problems: Too little water, direct sunlight and draughts will cause the leaves to wither and droop. Prone to common pests, especially red spider mite and mealy bug, and to fungus.

Aphelandra squarrosa
'Zebra Plant'

When in full bloom and healthy condition, this is one of the most arresting of our house plants. It earns its name from the cream-coloured stripes which follow the veins of the otherwise deep-green leaves. These leaves radiate from a thick central stem to form a bold, pyramid shape at the tip of which, during the autumn, the flower-head appears. This flower-head is a luxurious-looking affair, like a kind of art-deco lamp inspired by corn-on-the-cob, vivid yellow in colour. These are in fact bracts, or modified leaves, from which the real flowers – delicate little yellow trumpets – will emerge over a period of about six weeks.

These plants come originally from tropical Brazil and miss the steamy heat of the rainforests. They need careful attention, as a result of which they are frequently bought when in flower and subsequently discarded. It is, however, quite possible to nurture them from one year to the next, and certainly for a plant with such fine foliage it must surely be worth trying. The key is to supply enough light, warmth and humidity throughout the year; clip off the flower-heads when they begin to fade and prune vigorously in spring.

The most common variety available is the *Aphelandra squarrosa* 'Louisae', but there are several other varieties, including the *Aphelandra aurantica*, which has a scarlet flower-head.

Position: Plenty of light, but not direct sunlight. Avoid draughts.

Temperature: Keep between 60°F (16°C) and 75°F (24°C) when flowering: but the important thing is not to let the temperature fluctuate too much.

Water: Never allow the roots to dry out; keep the soil moist but do not stand in water. In high temperatures it is important to supply humidity by aerial-spraying, or by standing the pot on wet gravel, or by packing the pot in an outer container filled with damp peat, sand or moss.

Feeding: Once a fortnight, when flowering.

Propagation: Difficult: from new shoots in spring, with a propagator.

Soil: Standard loam-based compost.

Problems: Leaves wilting and dropping: too dry, too draughty. Rotting stem: too wet. Prone to common pests.

Aralia japonica

'False Castor Oil Plant' or 'Castor Oil Plant'

This is an elegant, deep-green plant with leaves that are reminiscent of the fig-leaves supposedly known to Adam and Eve, although in fact quite unrelated. The shiny leaves grow on long stems and form a bushy but airy concentration of foliage, sometimes over 3 ft (90 cm) tall.

As the Latin name suggests, this plant came originally from Japan which has a temperate climate similar to that of Europe. It has adapted easily enough, therefore, and is not difficult to keep.

There is a variegated form which has cream-coloured leaf-margins. There is also a fascinating variety of Aralia which has clusters of narrow, purple-green or bronze leaves with deeply serrated edges radiating from the tips of the stems, like shredded umbrellas. This is the *Aralia elegantissima*, or, to give its splendid alternative name, *Dizygotheca elegantissima*. It originates from the South Pacific and needs rather warmer and more humid conditions.

The *Aralia japonica* is also known as the *Fatsia japonica* or the *Aralia sieboldii*.

Position: Indirect light; will tolerate some direct sunlight. *Aralia japonica* seems to be happy enough in fairly dark conditions.
Temperature: Normal house temperatures are fine, although *Aralia elegantissima* needs to be kept above 60°F (16°C).
Water: Keep compost moist, but not wet, at all times. Supply humidity by aerial-spraying.
Feeding: Apply liquid feed once every two weeks in the summer.
Propagation: From stem-tip cuttings or shoots.
Soil: Standard potting compost.
Problems: Failure usually results from overwatering, or from exposing the plant to conditions that are too hot or dry. Prone to common pests.

Asparagus plumosus
'Asparagus Fern'

There are a number of members of the Asparagus family that provide us with excellent house plants. The best known is *Asparagus plumosus*, a fine and delicate-looking plant with a haze of tiny, needle-like leaves spread out on wiry stems in layers of horizontal triangles. It easily betrays its family connection to the edible Asparagus, which has similar foliage. These plants are popular with florists, who use sprigs of the foliage in bouquets and buttonholes; they are rather less popular with anyone who does the housework in a place where an Asparagus Fern has been neglected: when the tiny leaves fall, they get everywhere.

The other varieties include the *Asparagus densiflorus*

'Sprengeri', the Emerald Fern, which has rather more robust leaves like a kind of prickly grass, which spread forth and trail down in a bushy clump; and the even more robust-looking *Asparagus falcatus* with its more fleshy leaves growing on vertical, woody stems that can reach some 3 ft (90 cm) in height (beware of the thorns!)

All of these come from South Africa, but survive well in our climate. None of them are in fact ferns at all; nor are their leaves actually leaves, but modified branches.

Position: These plants prefer bright indirect light, but will tolerate quite shady positions.
Temperature: Normal room temperatures.
Water: Do not allow the plant to dry out. Water frequently in the summer, once a week in winter, and provide humidity by aerial-spraying.
Feeding: Use a mild mixture of plant food once a fortnight in summer.
Propagation: From seeds sown in the spring, in warm conditions; or by root division.
Soil: Standard potting compost.
Problems: Falling 'leaves': too hot or too dry. Prone to common pests, especially red spider mite and scale.

Aspidistra elatior
'Aspidistra' or 'Cast-Iron Plant'

Aspidistras are – at their best – elegant, spacious plants, with wide, lance-shaped leaves that stand tall on long, gently-arching stems. A rich, dark green in colour, these leaves have a striking texture on account of the veins that run the length of the leaf, giving a corrugated effect. There is also a rather lovely variegated form, with irregular creamy-white stripes following the lines of the veins.

The Aspidistra has earned its workaday common name, the Cast-Iron Plant, through its apparent indestructibility.

This, of all house plants, can survive the neglect to which most are subjected by their owners, a quality noted by the Victorians and the Edwardians in whose cold, smoke-filled and gas-lit homes survivors were few and far between. This accounts for the immense popularity which it enjoyed for over a half a century since its introduction from China in the mid-nineteenth century, and which ultimately led to its ridicule as the very symbol of middle-class respectability. George Orwell took up the theme in the title of his novel *Keep the Aspidistra Flying*, and of course the poor plant has been immortalized by the music hall song made famous by Gracie Fields, 'It's the B[-b-b-b-]iggest Aspidistra in the World'.

It is probably not so much this undeserved ignominy that accounts for the Aspidistra's comparative rarity these days

Aspidistra elatior

as the fact that these are slow-growing plants. Any plant that takes up more than an average amount of a grower's time and space will reach the market at a price that reflects this. This is a pity, because Aspidistras make fine house plants and deserve proper appreciation for their cast-iron constitutions.

If your Aspidistra produces a strange-looking growth at soil level, something like a tiny, open fig with a purple interior, do not be alarmed. This is the Aspidista's flower, a rare occurrence which will last no more than a day or two.

This is one of those foliage plants on which you should not use leaf-shine, a product that coats the leaves in a film of plastic to make them shiny. Use a damp sponge to keep the leaves clean.

Position: Can be very shady; avoid direct sunlight.
Temperature: Standard room temperatures.
Water: Likes plenty of water: water twice a week in summer; in winter keep watering to a minimum.
Feeding: Requires very little feeding: once every other month in summer; do not feed the variegated Aspidistra at all.
Propagation: By root division, or by potting up suckers (shoots growing at the base of the plant).
Soil: Standard potting compost.
Problems: Brown patches on leaves: too much sunlight. Leaves splitting: too much plant-food. Prone to common pests.

Asplenium nidus avis
'Bird's Nest Fern'

This is one of the most attractive ferns – although it does not have the familiar, shredded fronds that are commonly associated with ferns. Instead, it has glossy, green leaves that unfurl from a central rosette: these leaves have a watery freshness about them, and when light passes through them, they show their beautiful translucent qualities, like a kind of green alabaster.

The Bird's Nest Fern comes from the tropical part of northern Australia, where it can grow leaves of some 5 ft (1.5 m) in length. Our homes could not hope to imitate the conditions required for such growth, even if we wanted it, but none the less this plant, whatever its size, does need warmth and humidity to thrive.

There is another member of the Asplenium family that is used as a house plant: the *Asplenium bulbiferum*, which comes from New Zealand. It looks rather like a large parsley plant, and grows to some 2 ft (60 cm) tall. A notable aspect of this plant is that its young grow as tiny plantlets on the fronds of the mother-plant, giving rise to its common names: the Mother Fern, or the more picturesque Hen-and-Chickens Fern.

Position: Bright indirect light.
Temperature: Standard room temperatures, but do not allow winter temperatures to drop below 60°F (16°C).
Water: Keep moist at all times. Humidity is important: supply by aerial-spraying, or stand the pot on wet gravel, or pack the pot in an outer container filled with damp peat, sand or moss.
Feeding: Use a mild mixture of plant food when watering during the summer.
Propagation: From spores, if kept warm and humid; in the case of *Asplenium bulbiferum*, from the plantlets on the fronds.
Soil: Standard peat-based compost.
Problems: Dry, brown patches on leaves: too dry and hot, or too cold. Pale leaves: too much sunlight.

Azalea
'Azalea'

The tiny, neatly-clipped Azalea bushes that are brought into the shops towards Christmas provide a wonderful show of colour at a time when winter is taking away the last tinges of autumn. Pink, red, white and orange, single and double blooms – these are set off against the deep-green foliage to make handsome plants that will stay in flower for several weeks, and which, by careful treatment, can be made to repeat the performance the following year.

Azaleas have been re-classified so that they now form part of the Rhododendron family. The variety that is brought in at Christmas is the *Rhododendron simsii*, known as the Indian Azalea but which in fact – just to make matters really confusing – comes from China. There is also another variety called *Rhododendron obtusum* which originated in Japan and which has smaller flowers that bloom in the early spring.

Azaleas are not easy subjects to look after, since they are fussy about room temperature (which should be only moderately warm) and need plenty of humidity. This is why many people will keep an Azalea when it is in flower, and then discard it. This, however, does not have to be an Azalea's fate: after flowering, the plant can be moved to a cooler position, pruned back and kept moist until spring. It can then be planted out in the garden, pot and all. If kept well-watered and humid over the summer, and brought into the house before the first frosts, trimmed, fed and kept warm, it has every chance of rewarding you with another fine show of winter flowers.

Position: Ideally, plenty of indirect light with some hours of sunlight every day. Keep away from radiators or cold windows.

Temperature: Not much higher than 60°F (16°C), dropping to 50°F (10°C) at night.

Water: The plant must be watered thoroughly each time: if possible, plunge the pot into water and immerse it; retain it there until the bubbles stop coming out (when this happens it has been adequately watered); drain well. Azaleas need plenty of water when in flower, but note that they detest lime, so use rainwater if you intend to keep the plant from year to year. Provide humidity every day by aerial-spraying; again use rainwater for this, or filtered water, otherwise the lime may cause brown spots to appear on the flowers. Humidity would also be improved by standing the pot on a base of wet gravel.

Feeding: Use liquid plant-food when the plant is growing in the summer, and when flowering in winter.

Propagation: From stem cuttings in early summer. When the new growth is about 3 in (8 cm) long, stem cuttings will root easily in half peat, half sharp sand if kept warm.

Soil: Standard peat-based compost.

Problems: Most problems are caused by lack of humidity and too much warmth. Overwatering will cause the buds to fall before flowering. Prone to common pests.

Begonia Rex

'Foliage Begonia'

Begonias form a huge genus of plants – some 900 species in all. Those that serve as house plants are divided into two main groups: the Foliage Begonias and the Flowering Begonias. Both groups have one distinguishing peculiarity in common: their curious, pointed leaves that curve away from the off-centre point where they are joined to the stalk, like the first steps of a spiral staircase. This is a living Paisley pattern: and the foliage varieties in particular have been specially developed to create these bold arabesques with their extraodinary leaves.

There is a huge range of Foliage Begonias, each with its distinctive appeal. *Begonia rex* comes in a number of forms, with mat-finish leaves in combinations of red, green, brown, cream and green; the leaves are usually at least 6 in (15 cm) long, heavily-contoured and with serrated edges, and form a bold clump of foliage. *Begonia boweri* 'Tiger' is a much more compact variety, with smaller leaves of only 1 in (25 mm) or so, light-green, mottled with red along the veins; tiny hairs grow along the leaf margins and on the pink-spotted, fleshy stems. The *Begonia maculata*, on the other hand, has large, leathery leaves up to about 8 in (20 cm) in length, growing spaciously on cane-like stems, with hundreds of iridescent white spots set off against a dark-green background, and blushing red undersides. There are many others – names such as Iron Cross Begonia and Metallic Leaf Begonia tell of their distinguishing leaf-markings.

Many of these Begonias are hybrids, bred from ancestors that came from tropical lands around the world. Despite their origins, however, they do not require any very special conditions and are easy enough to grow. Their name, incidentally, refers to a seventeenth-century French botanist called Michel Begon.

Position: Plenty of indirect light; not bright sunlight.
Temperature: Standard room temperatures; not happy in temperatures below 60°F (16°C) in winter.
Water: Keep just moist all the year, and do not let the plant stand in water.
Feeding: Feed every two weeks during the summer.
Propagation: From leaf cuttings pinned to soil and kept warm, or leaf-and-stem cuttings rooted in water, or by root-division.
Soil: Standard peat-based compost.
Problems: Begonias do not like conditions that are either too hot and dry, or too cold, but overwatering is probably the biggest threat, provoking rot and mildew. Cut back and treat a damaged plant and adjust watering and position.

Begonia semperflorens
'Flowering Begonia'

There are numerous types of Flowering Begonia of which the *Begonia semperflorens*, or Wax Begonia, is but one, albeit probably the most common. *Semperflorens* means 'ever-flowering', and indeed this plant will produce its red, pink, orange or white flowers almost all year long if given the right conditions. These are lovely plants, often bought when in full flower; sad, therefore, that so often they wilt and collapse within days of coming into the house. They should be simple enough to keep, but it seems only too easy to overindulge them with moisture, which rapidly brings rot and mildew in its wake.

There are a number of other varieties of Flowering Begonia, with distinctive flowers and foliage. *Begonia cheimantha*, the Lorraine Begonia, and *Begonia hiemalis* are two others commonly found, and modern hybrids of these can flower throughout the year. There are other, more specialist varieties, with large double-blooms that last through the late summer, such as the tuber-rooted *Begonia tuberhybrida*.

Position: Plenty of light, although *Begonia semperflorens* will grow happily on a north-facing windowsill in the summer months, ensure some sunlight during the winter.

Temperature: Standard room temperatures, but not below 50°F (10°C) in winter.

Water: Keep on the dry side, watering to the base of the pot, once a week in summer, less often in winter. They do like some humidity, but this is best provided by standing the plant on wet gravel as aerial-spraying can mark the flowers and might provoke rot.

Feeding: Feed every two weeks when in flower.

Propagation: From seed or from stem cuttings in spring; both will need warmth. It is a wise precaution to propagate from cuttings regularly, given the high incidence of failure in these plants.

Soil: Standard peat-based potting compost.

Problems: Mildew and rot are the greatest threats, usually provoked by not watering to the plant's base, overwatering, or excessive humidity. Dry, brown patches on the edges of the leaves: too hot and dry. Prone to common pests.

Beloperone guttata

'Shrimp Plant'

The soft leaves and beautifully-shaded flower-heads of the Shrimp Plant make this one of the most gentle and pleasing of all house plants. For once the common name is entirely apt: the flowers – little white trumpets – grow from a cluster of scale-like bracts (modified leaves) which flop over in limp curves to resemble the body of a shrimp, complete with legs and feelers.

Shrimp plants will form tidy little bushes if kept under control by pruning back after flowering has finished: if they grow much larger than a 6 in (15 cm) hemisphere they rapidly become rather leggy and lose their peculiarly soft charm. It is the bracts that give them their distinctive colour: these are usually in gradated shades of bronze and light green, but some forms have all-yellow bracts. They will flower during the summer months only; when not in flower they are not very spectacular, and will be happy to rest in a cool room. They come originally from Mexico and like plenty of sun, but they do not seem to miss the warmth of their native climate, provided that the room temperature is kept fairly constant.

This plant is sometimes confused with the *Pachystachys lutea*, known to some as the Golden Shrimp Plant; it has similarly-formed bracts, but is rather different overall.

Position: Plenty of light, even direct sunlight: the more light, the more colourful the bracts.
Temperature: Normal room temperatures are fine, but should not drop below 50°F (10°C) in winter.
Water: Water well when growing in summer, but make sure the soil is well-drained so that it can dry out between waterings.
Feeding: Feed once every two weeks in the summer.
Propagation: From stem-tip cuttings in spring, with warmth and humidity.
Soil: Standard loam-based potting compost.
Problems: Leaves yellowing and dropping: too dry and cold, or too wet. Bracts not taking on colour: not enough light. Plant becomes leggy: prune back and keep pinching out growing tips. Prone to common pests.

Caladium bicolor

'Angel Wings' or 'Elephant's Ears'

This is one of the most prized of the foliage house plants, for its leaves have quite exceptional markings. There are a number of hybrid forms, each with its own predominant range of colours, but they all have one thing in common: spectacular colour arrangements. Imagine crossing an ordinance-survey map with a spider's web, and then intensifying the colours and this will give you some idea. In

Caladium bicolor

most hybrids the veins are picked out in one colour, while the surface of the leaf is covered in fairly symmetrical patterns of other colours – usually combinations of red, green and white, and also sometimes pink. The distribution of colour on each leaf may vary widely on any single plant.

The common names refer to the size of the leaves, which can be up to 18 in (45 cm) in length, although the plant itself will be not much taller than this. When young, the leaves are rather smaller, so that a mature plant will often have a somewhat top-heavy look. The leaves are shaped like an arrowhead, basically triangular with the leaf-stalk joining the leaf at the tip of a deep triangular indent.

Angel Wings come from Brazil, where they are used to the steamy heat of the tropical rainforests. Unfortunately they still need similar conditions and, expensive though they are, they are very hard to keep from one year to the next. After the summer the plants will die down and the tubers (the underground stems which produce the buds) have to be stored carefully in dry peat over the winter if they are to come to life again the next spring; this really needs hothouse conditions. They are therefore usually treated as summer visitors to our houses and regretfully discarded at the end of the season.

The Caladiums are members of the Arum family. The species that comes to us as a house plant is the *Caladium bicolor*, also known as *Caladium hortulanum*. Hybrids range from 'Candidum', which has white leaves with green veins, to 'Frieda Hemple', with green leaf-margins surrounding a bold, red heart shape – and all kinds of variations on these themes in between.

Position: Bright indirect light; avoid direct sunlight.
Temperature: Must be at least 60°F (16°C).
Water: Plenty of water when growing, easing off as the plant reaches maturity; humidity is best supplied by placing the pot on a base of wet gravel.
Feeding: Feed once every three weeks when growing.
Propagation: By dividing the tubers in spring; they require plenty of warmth (around 70°F or 21°C). Not easy.
Soil: A mixture of standard loam-based potting compost and moss peat, in equal parts.
Problems: Lack of warmth and humidity causes the leaves to droop and go brown. Coloration will be lost if the plant does not receive enough light. Prone to mildew and common pests.

Campanula isophylla
'Italian Bellflower' or 'Star of Bethlehem'

This is a delightful flowering house plant, and one of the easiest to grow. It has abundant clusters of white or pale-mauve, star-shaped flowers that tumble down the edge of a pot, seeking the light. The leaves are heart-shaped, the size of a thumbnail, growing on brittle stems filled with a milky sap.

Campanulas will flower throughout most of the latter part of the growing year. If you return from holiday to find your plant drooping for lack of water, it will greet your return by reviving quickly when the drought ends. However, such events are best avoided, as lack of water will usually cause the lower leaves on the trailing stems to die

off, making the plant leggy and unsightly. You can trim off the dead leaves but this requires some patience, as it is only too easy to trim away flower-bearing stems at the same time. It is advisable to keep picking off the flowers as they fade: this will promote the growth of further flowers and keep the plant tidy.

Campanula isophylla

Campanulas come from the Northern Mediterranean, so they adapt well to the temperate climates of our households. Flowering will cease as winter tightens its grip; the plants will survive to another year if kept moist over the winter. They are, in addition, very easy to propagate.

Position: Plenty of light, but keep out of direct sunlight, especially in summer.

Temperature: Standard room temperatures are fine.

Water: Keep well-watered when growing and flowering; keep moist in winter. They like a little humidity: the atmosphere of a kitchen or bathroom is quite adequate; aerial-spraying may mark the flowers.

Feeding: Once a month when growing and flowering.

Propagation: From stem-tip cuttings placed directly into damp compost in spring.

Soil: Standard loam-based potting compost.

Problems: Leaves and flowers wilting and turning brown: too little water. Overwatering will cause rot and collapse.

Capsicum annuum

'Ornamental Chilli Pepper' or 'Christmas Pepper'

These plants always inspire a sense of wonder when they come into the shops as winter closes in: with their bright-green bushes of fine, pointed leaves crowned with clusters of tiny chilli peppers – yellow, orange and red – pointing skywards, they bridge the gap between the fading autumn colours outside and the red and evergreen colours of Christmas.

These plants are annuals: they will only survive a single season, fruiting just once from autumn to around the New Year and thereby providing the seeds for another genera-tion before fading away. Those producing the characteristic cone-shaped peppers are the most common varieties: the peppers are green when they first appear, maturing through yellow to red, or, as in the hybrid 'Christmas Greeting', to purple.

These fruits are edible, but very, very hot: if you are tempted to try, do not just bite into the pepper but cut it with a knife and test its strength by appplying a tiny amount of juice to the tip of your tongue. This will tell you whether you wish to proceed any further! But here is another warning: you must be careful that you have indeed got a chilli plant, and not the *Solanum capsicastrum* or Winter Cherry, which comes into the shops at about the same time as the chilli plants. The Winter Cherry has round fruits, a little like miniature oranges: these are poisonous and can cause bad stomach upsets. Children, of course, should not be tempted by either.

Chilli plants came originally from the tropical lands of Central and South America and only became known to the world at large after the great Age of Discovery took European explorers to the Americas in the late fifteenth century. It is interesting, therefore, to reflect that the cookery of South East Asia and India had to await the introduction of chilli peppers from the Americas in subsequent centuries before it could develop the fiery qualities for which we know it today.

Position: Plenty of light, ideally with some sunlight during the day.
Temperature: Keep warm, certainly above 60°F (16°C).
Water: Water well when growing; reduce watering when in full fruit. It likes some humidity, especially in hot, dry conditions: supply this by aerial-spraying.
Feeding: Feed once a week when growing, but not when in full fruit.
Propagation: From seed in spring, in a propagator; not easy.
Soil: Standard loam-based compost.
Problems: The plant will not be happy if either too hot and dry, or too wet and cold: the leaves will wilt and drop. Prone to common pests.

Chlorophytum comosum
'Spider Plant' or 'St Bernard's Lily'

Anyone who has ever kept house plants must at one stage have owned a Spider Plant. It is the perfect beginner's plant and almost impossible to demolish, even by the usually deadly combinations of maltreatment and neglect: if you cannot keep a Spider Plant maybe you should take up another hobby – piano-smashing, for instance.

This is not to say that Spider Plants actually like being mistreated: common though they are, these are beautiful plants that will only be at their best if given a little care. They do, after all, come from Southern Africa and have had only a century to adapt to our less clement temperatures. They are grown primarily for their foliage – thin, lance-like leaves that arch outwards from a central rosette, creating exuberant, architectural shapes. This is the kind of plant that deserves to be in a hanging basket, or at least placed high in a room, for its graceful curves are best appreciated from below. The form that one usually comes across is the *Chlorophytum comosum* 'Variegatum', which has cream or white stripes running the full length of the leaves and green leaf-margins, and sometimes the reverse of this.

A mature plant will produce long, tough shoots from the rosette from time to time. The tips of these will bud and produce a sparse group of small but pretty white flowers with yellow centres. These shoots will later produce plantlets, which will stay on the stem until they are given a chance to take root in soil. If they become untidy, they can be clipped off without harming the mother plant. The plantlets grow so easily and so well that most Spider Plants in homes today probably come from cuttings from plants belonging to friends and relatives.

Chlorophytum comosum

Unhealthy Spider Plants are not attractive: when they go limp or when the tips of the leaves dry out and go brown, they lose their arching beauty. This is perfectly avoidable if one is prepared to give them plenty of water whenever they show signs of wilting, and a regular dose of fertilizer in the summer. They show their gratitude by reviving quickly. Quite how undemanding they are can be seen from the fact that they appear to require almost no soil at all: often a perfectly healthy plant will crack open its plastic pot, revealing a solid block of spaghetti-like roots which have done the damage quite simply because they had no other place to go.

Position: This plant will tolerate as shady a position as any house plant, but is happier in bright indirect light. It needs some light to maintain its leaf-colour.

Temperature: Standard room temperatures are fine.

Water: Water well at intervals, especially during the summer; you can allow the plant to dry out between waterings, but water as soon as it shows signs of wilting. Humidity will be welcomed when conditions are hot and dry: this is a plant that does well in the humid atmosphere of a kitchen or bathroom.

Feeding: Feed every other week during the summer.

Propagation: From the plantlets that grow on the shoots, placed in damp compost.

Soil: Standard loam-based potting compost.

Problems: Tips of leaves going brown: plant needs more moisture or humidity. Pale leaves: not enough light, or needs feeding. Prone to common pests.

Cissus antarctica
'Kangaroo Vine'

This is a fine-looking and useful vine: with its highly tolerant and undemanding nature it earns a well-deserved place in our homes which only too frequently do not have enough well-lit spots to grow many of the more flamboyant house plants.

The mature leaves of the Kangaroo Vine are dark-green, with gently toothed edges; young leaves are a lighter, fresher green with slightly wetter-looking shine. As with other vines, the Kangaroo Vine has tendrils that will clasp on to a support – although sometimes they need a bit of encouragement to do this. In the right conditions, and with suitable supports, it can grow some 10 ft (3 m) high.

No prizes for guessing that this plant comes from Australia – although the common name seems to be no more than a broad association with the plant's origins. There are several other varieties of Cissus vine available. A common one is the *Rhoicissus rhomboidea*, sometimes known as the Natal Vine in reference to its South African origins, and also known as Grape Ivy, which is misleading since it is not an ivy at all. This is very similar in all ways to the Kangaroo Vine, except that its leaves grow in threes, in a kind of heart-shaped trefoil. *Cissus striata*, from Chile, is a trailing plant with delicate leaves divided into five leaflets. *Cissus discolor* is somewhat different from its cousins: it has basically green leaves, with a crinkled surface, with great splashes of white in the areas between the veins, like a light covering of snow on a range of hills; these colours are further offset by touches of pink on the leaf surface, and ruby-red undersides. Confusingly, this plant has the common name of Begonia Vine; coming from South East Asia, it requires rather warmer and more humid conditions than the Kangaroo Vine and is rather less easy to keep.

Rhoicissus rhomboidea

Position: A fairly shady position is quite acceptable; keep out of bright sunlight.
Temperature: Normal room temperatures, but *Cissus discolor* should be kept at temperatures above 65°F (18°C).
Water: Keep moist at all times. All the Cissus vines like humidity, but it is only absolutely vital for the *Cissus discolor*, which should be sprayed with water every day.
Feeding: Feed once a fortnight during the summer.
Propagation: From stem-tip cuttings in compost.

Soil: Standard loam-based compost.
Problems: Dry, brown spots on leaves: overwatering.
Leaves dry out: too hot and dry. Prone to common pests.

Codiaeum variegatum

'Croton' or 'Joseph's Coat'

Crotons are splendidly colourful plants, as the alternative
common name suggests: their strong, thick leaves are
painted in a frenzy of colours – red, yellow, orange and
green in splashes, stripes and patches. The most widely-
known variety is the *Codiaeum variegatum pictum*, but
there are a large number of other varieties, each distin-
guished by their particular coloration and leaf-shapes:
forked, ribbon-like, broad or pencil-thin, frilly-edged or
smooth.

These plants originally came from South East Asia.
They are a good example of the work that nurseries have
done to adapt exotic plants to the variable conditions of
our homes, since for a long while after this plant was
introduced it was considered to be too tender for any
conditions outside the hothouse. Now, however, more
tolerant characteristics have been bred into these plants,
and they can withstand a much broader range of
temperature. That said, however, they will not be happy
in temperatures that drop below 55°F (13°C), and a cold
winter is quite likely to see them off.

Crotons grow quickly and can easily become straggly if
there is only one stem, especially if leaves are lost to the
climate. To make a more bushy plant, pinch out the
growing tip of the stem in spring: this will encourage side
shoots. The growing tip can be used to propagate other
plants – but be sure to stop the flow of sap with powdered
charcoal or petroleum jelly, otherwise the plant could be
seriously weakened.

Position: As much light as possible, but not direct sunlight. Crotons must have good light to maintain their distinctive colours.

Temperature: Ideally somewhere between 60°F (16°C) and 75°F (24°C); the real trick, however, is to keep the temperature as constant as possible within these limits.

Water: Keep moist at all times; supply plenty of water in the summer. Crotons like humidity: spray with water daily, or alternatively stand the pot on a base of wet gravel.

Feeding: Feed once every two months during the growing period in spring and summer.

Propagation: From stem-tip cuttings, ideally with a propagator; or by air-layering.

Soil: Standard loam-based potting compost.

Problems: Falling leaves: too cold or too dry, or temperatures are fluctuating too much. Poor coloration in leaves: not enough light. Prone to common pests.

Coleus blumei

'Coleus' or 'Flame Nettle'

These are handsome plants, grown for their colourful foliage which is usually green and red in varying proportions, but numerous hybrids have exploited a range of other colours, mixing in pink, yellow, cream and grey. The common name Flame Nettle describes them well: their serrated leaves are similar to, if somewhat larger than, those of the common nettle, and the plants have a similar overall shape – but there is no fear being stung! On the contrary, the soft, mat textures and crinkly contours of the leaves give them a welcoming and comfortable look. Some hybrid forms, such as 'Sabre' and 'Firebird', have more marked indentations in the leaf-edge, more like an oak leaf than the leaf of a nettle.

Coleus plants are really annuals and cannot be expected

to last from year to year. To keep them in shape during the growing season, pinch out the growing tips and remove any flowers that appear.

The plants will become tired and unsightly as the year draws to a close; this is the time to act boldly and do away with them, unless you wish to try to nurture them through the winter so that cuttings can be taken in spring, which can then be used to create fresh plants for another season.

Position: Plenty of light, even direct sun, provided that it does not scorch the plant through a window in summer.
Temperature: Standard room temperatures. To take a Coleus through the winter, temperatures of at least 60°F (16°C) will be needed.
Water: Water well during the summer.
Feeding: No fertilizer is required; if applied to young plants it may encourage their leaves to revert to green.
Propagation: From seed or from stem-tip cuttings.
Soil: Standard peat-based compost
Problems: Leaves shrivel and drop: too hot and dry, or the end of the season. Pale coloration or leaves reverting to green: not enough light, or may require feeding, or both. Prone to common pests, particularly greenfly.

Cordyline terminalis

'Cordyline'

The Cordyline is just the sort of plant to benefit from the great revival of the use of house plants as an integral part of interior design. As offices, banks, hotels and restaurants look for specimens that have a scale, elegance and lushness to bring the right touch of nature to large architectural spaces, Cordylines – along with the Dracaenas (with which they are often confused), Yuccas, and others that make up the informal group known as the 'false palms' – come into their own.

These plants do indeed need space: they grow to about 2 ft (60 cm) tall, with broad, tongue-like leaves arching upwards and outwards from a central stem with the shape, if not the texture, of a feather duster. As they grow older, the lower leaves will drop off, creating a palm-like trunk (hence the term 'false palm'), but this will take several years as Cordylines will only grow some 6 in (15 cm) a year. As with most plants that are slow-growers, the larger, more impressive ones are rather expensive, but you can buy Cordylines when they are very small, and, with patience and regular repotting, nurture them to their full glory over the years.

Cordyline terminalis

Most varieties on the market have striking leaf-markings. Two in particular stand out: the *Cordyline terminalis* 'Tricolor', with its green leaves splashed with cream, red and pink; and *Cordyline terminalis* 'Red Edge', with its deep-green leaves and bright-red leaf margins.

The Cordylines come from the tropical and temperate zones of South America, Australasia and Polynesia; they are not difficult to grow but do require some protection from the cold.

Position: Plenty of light, even direct sunlight, provided that it is not at its full strength in the summer. Brightly-coloured Cordylines will revert to green if kept away from good light.

Temperature: Try to keep the temperature above 65°F (18°C) in winter; otherwise normal room temperatures are fine.

Water: Water well in summer, but do not allow the pot to stand in water; reduce watering in winter to keep soil just moist; never allow the soil to dry out. Humidity is important, especially in hot, dry conditions; supply this by aerial-spraying (but not in direct sunlight), and by placing the pot on a base of wet gravel.

Feeding: Feed mature plants every three months.

Propagation: From stem-tip cuttings, suckers (shoots that grow at the base of the plant) and stem sections, kept warm and humid.

Soil: Standard potting compost.

Problems: Leaves drying out and dropping: too hot and dry, not enough humidity. Leaves limp and drooping: too much water. Poor coloration: not enough light. Prone to common pests.

Crassula argentea

'Jade Plant' or 'Money Tree'

This is an unspectacular plant, but a sturdy friend. It will grow slowly but steadily, and is not vindictive if neglected. Both the common names are appropriate: there is something rather stone like about these plants, with their woody stems and small, succulent leaves, reminding us perhaps of the miniature Japanese *bonsai* trees, or even those Japanese ornaments which imitate *bonsai* trees in wood and wire and coloured glass. As for money, the leaves do have the compact feel of coins: total neglect will result in a windfall, as the plant uses up the moisture stored in the leaves and discards them, leaving a bare, scarred stem.

Jade plants can grow to a considerable size over the years: in places such as California, where they are grown outdoors in gardens, they have to be rigorously controlled to prevent them taking over. In our homes they will need to be trimmed from time to time to give them a good shape. In a mature plant tiny roots will sprout underneath the leaves: propagation is simply a question of cutting off a section with roots and placing it in damp compost.

Although originally from Africa and the Middle East, the Jade Plant is very easy to grow and requires little light to survive, although in very poor light it will start to produce leggy shoots with tiny leaves that ruin the shape of the plant. The leaves have a kind of silvery scale on them, giving rise to another common name, Silvery Succulent, this scale collects dust, which then has to be rather carefully and laboriously cleaned off to keep the plant attractive and healthy: the easiest solution is to take the plant outside on a mild day and hose it down gently, or to stand it out of doors for the summer, where it will enjoy the fresh air and summer rains.

Crassula argentea

The Crassulas include a variety of other succulent plants; the *Crassula arborescens*, with its grey-green leaves, is similar to the Jade Plant, but the others are so different as to make one wonder that they belong to the same genus at all. The common names are an indication of this: *Crassula lycopodioides*, the Rat Tail Plant, and *Crassula perforata*, the String of Buttons, for example.

The Jade Plant, *Crassula argentea*, is sometimes known as *Crassula obliqua* or *Crassula portulacea*.

Position: Plenty of indirect light, and even direct sunlight, but this plant is happy enough in shady conditions away from a window.

Temperature: Standard room temperatures are fine.

Water: Water when the soil becomes dry. Succulents have

evolved their fleshy leaves and stems to cope with drought.

Feeding: Feed mature plants once every three months.

Propagation: From stem-cuttings, ideally when roots are already present.

Soil: Standard loam-based potting compost.

Problems: Falling leaves: too dry. Spindly, light-green shoots: not enough light.

Cyclamen persicum

'Cyclamon'

Surely one of the most delightful of all the flowering house plants, the Cyclamen is a great favourite, bringing colour and elegance into our homes from autumn through to early spring – if properly cared for. From the sturdy clumps of

Cyclamen persicum

curly, heart-shaped leaves, with their gently serrated edges, rise the flowers on their long stems: pink, white, red or purple. They have unique lines, the six petals pulled back from the central trumpet, as though they were designed to move at speed – like the winged sandals of Mercury, or a whippet with its ears turned back for the chase. The flowers unfurl from buds that first appear on the stems as tightly-rolled spirals; it is these that give rise to the Cyclamen's name, from the Greek *kyklos*, a circle.

Cyclamens came originally from the Mediterranean region, and so they are used to a temperate climate: they do not need hothouse conditions, and suffer if kept too warm. They also suffer if not correctly watered: the key to success is providing the correct supply of moisture. The soil must never be allowed to dry out, but water must not be left to settle around the corm from which the plant grows: this causes the rotting that is the fate of so many fine Cyclamens. The best solution is to supply water to the base of the pot only. To provide the humidity essential to this plant in centrally-heated homes, stand the pot on a base of wet gravel; aerial-spraying will damage the flowers and can cause rot.

The flowers will last for some two to three months; pluck the stems out as each flower fades to encourage the growth of the new flowers. Eventually the plant will reach the end of its season and start to die back; it is often discarded at this stage, but if you have the room and the inclination, you can keep the corm to flower the following year. Let the plant dry out gradually as the leaves turn yellow; keep the soil just moist in the spring; in late spring or early summer, after the last frost, plant the corm and its pot in a shaded part of the garden and allow it to grow until September, watering it during any dry spells. Then repot it in fresh compost, keep it carefully watered, and bring it back into the house as the flower buds develop.

There are now numerous Cyclamen hybrids available, all developed from the original wild *Cyclamen persicum*: each has its own particular characteristics, such as the colour of its flowers, its flowering season and leaf-markings. The hybrid 'Decora', for instance, has broad silver-grey borders running right round the leaf-margins. Standard varieties grow to some 12 in (30 cm) tall, dwarf varieties to some 6 in (15 cm).

Position: Bright indirect light.
Temperature: Cool room temperatures, not above 65°F (18°C); be sure to protect the plant from extreme cold or frost.
Water: Keep moist when growing and in flower: supply

water to the base of the pot only; use lime-free water for preference. Humidity should be supplied by standing the pot on a base of wet gravel; or place the pot in an outer container of damp peat, sand or moss.

Feeding: Feed once a fortnight when growing and when flowering.

Propagation: From seed in spring; or by dividing the corm when it has budded (each division must have two or three 'eyes' on it).

Soil: Standard loam-based or peat-based potting compost.

Problems: Cyclamens will droop and fade if kept too hot and dry. Complete collapse is almost inevitable if rot gets into the corm because of overwatering. Prone to mildew and greenfly.

Cyperus diffusus
'Umbrella Plant' or 'Papyrus Plant'

This is an elegant and interesting plant that grows to anything from 2 ft (60 cm) to 4 ft (120 cm) tall, with long, thin, straight stems, at the end of which are sprays of leaves radiating from the tip like the ribs of an umbrella – hence the name.

Cyperus diffusus and its smaller cousin *Cyperus alternifolius* are both called Umbrella Plants. The term Papyrus Plant is commonly used, but is in fact incorrect, as this refers to the rather larger *Cyperus papyrus*, with its bushy head, like a horse-tail fly-whisk. This is the plant that grows profusely on the banks of the River Nile and which was stripped and pummelled into sheets by the Ancient Egyptians to make a form of paper which we call 'papyrus' and which gave us the word 'paper'. However, the true Papyrus Plant is too demanding and ungainly for the average home.

Umbrella Plants come from Madagascar, where they

grow in conditions similar to those on the banks of the Nile. These too are water plants, and love to have lashings of water all the time: here is a plant that you cannot overwater! It will also survive short periods of drying out, but then the humidity will also be low and the leaves will start to turn yellow and dry up.

One of the curious features of these plants is that the young grow from the leaf-heads. When the plant decides it is time to produce another generation, the long stems will bow and then bend, lowering the leaf-head to the ground. In the wild this would mean that the leaf-head would now trail in the muddy water. Before long roots will grow from the centre of the leaf-head, and another plant will come into being.

Cyperus alternifolius

This habit makes the Umbrella Plant one of the easiest to propagate; but it also means that it is apt to look rather untidy when it decides to make a bid for propagation of its own accord.

From time to time flowers will appear between the leaves at the tips of some of the stems: small and dirty-white on the end of spindly stems, they are not particularly special but do add an extra touch of exuberance to this explosive looking plant.

Position: Will tolerate fairly shady conditions, but does best in good, indirect light, with some sunlight during the day.

Temperature: Standard room temperatures are fine; avoid temperatures below 50°F (10°C) in winter.

Water: Keep constantly watered – as much water as you like!

Feeding: Add a mild mixture of plant food to the water once a week during the summer.

Propagation: From a leaf-head rooted in water and then potted in compost.

Soil: Standard loam-based compost.

Problems: Leaves going dry and brown: not enough water or, in winter, too cold. Prone to whitefly.

Dieffenbachia picta

'Leopard Lily' or 'Dumb Cane'

This is another member of the Arum family which traces its ancestry back to tropical Brazil, although it is named after Dr Dieffenbach, a German botanist. With its rich, elegant leaves in light green and creams forming an abundant mass of foliage, it gives the impression of cool, healthy vigour, earning it increasing popularity in recent years. It is usually sold under the picturesque name of Leopard Lily: the less marketable title of Dumb Cane refers to the fact that the sap is poisonous and can inflame the mouth and throat seriously if consumed. It is wise precaution, therefore, to wash your hands after handling this plant.

The Leopard Lily will grow fast in the right conditions, increasing in height by as much as 1 ft (30 cm) in a year. New leaves emerge from the growing tip in the form of a tightly-coiled spiral; the older the plant, the larger the leaves, reaching as much as 18 in (45 cm) in length. It does not require any very special treatment, although it must have a reasonable amount of light to maintain its distinctive leaf-markings, and requires careful watering and some humidity. Eventually the lower leaves will drop off and a trunk will form at the base of the plant, the reason for which the Dieffenbachias have a place in the informal group called 'false palms'. This can make the Leopard Lily look rather ungainly and, after four years or so, it may be avisable to cut it back and use the shoots to start afresh.

Dieffenbachia picta is the variety that provides the most splendid leaf-designs, with hybrids such as 'Rudolf Roehrs' banishing green to a mere token gesture around the edge of an otherwise silvery-cream leaf. Other species include the elegant, but less variegated *Dieffenbachia amoena*, which has rather larger leaves than the *Dieffenbachia picta*.

Position: Bright indirect light.

Temperature: Needs to be kept fairly warm: do not let winter temperatures drop below 60°F (16°C).

Water: Wait until the compost is almost dry before watering, then add water until it drains out through the bottom of the pot. Humidity is important: supply this by aerial-spraying or by standing the pot on a base of wet gravel, or by packing the pot in an outer container filled with damp peat, sand or moss.

Feeding: Feed mature plants with a mild mixture of plant food once every three months.

Propagation: From suckers (shoots growing at the base of the plant); or from stem sections, kept warm and damp; or by air-layering.

Soil: Standard loam-based potting compost.

Problems: Leaves dropping: too cold or too draughty. Leaves going yellow and dropping: too much water. Prone to common pests.

Dracaena marginata

'Dracaena' or 'Madagascar Dragon Tree'

The Dracaenas form an important section within the informal group known as 'false palms'. These are spectacular plants, bursting forth from a central rosette in a spray of strap-like foliage; as they get older, the lower leaves drop off, leaving a woody trunk rather like that of a palm. Although when small these are standard-sized house plants, large versions on tall trunks can reach some 10 ft (3 m) high and can have all the presence of small trees. As with many of the 'false palms', particularly the Cordylines with which they are often confused, Dracaenas have become increasingly popular as plants for offices and restaurants, where they can be properly displayed in all their impressive elegance. To meet the demand for mature plants, growers will use a technique whereby a young shoot is inserted into the top of long section of living trunk or cane, or sometimes the canes themselves are made to produce shoots by being brought on under glass. These so-called Ti-trees make tall and impressive plants, albeit with a slightly amputated look about them.

This is another example of a plant that has benefited from the hard work of growers over the decades, who have succeeded in turning a tropical plant from Africa and Asia into one that can tolerate conditions that usually prevail in the home. A number of varieties are available, including the variegated *Dracaena schryveriana* with cream leaf-margins, and the splendid *Dracaena marginata* 'Tricolor' with narrow leaves of green and yellow and pink leaf-margins.

Position: Bright indirect light.
Temperature: Standard room temparatures; ideally winter temperatures should not drop below 65°F (18°C), but the more robust varieties will survive 55°F (13°C).
Water: Keep the soil moist: never let it dry out, nor let the plant stand in water for any length of time. Supply humidity by aerial-spraying every other day in hot, dry conditions, and if possible place the pot on a base of wet gravel.
Feeding: Feed once a month with a mild mixture of plant food during the summer.
Propagation: From stem cuttings, or from suckers (shoots

growing at the base of the plant), or by air-layering; requires warmth and humidity.

Soil: Standard loam-based potting compost.

Problems: Leaves falling: too hot and dry. New leaves crinkled and sickly: needs feeding. Drooping leaves and rot: too much water. Prone to common pests.

Erica hyemalis
'French Heather' or 'Cape Heath'

As its name suggests, this is a relative of the rugged heathers that grow across the moorlands of northern England and Scotland. It is similar in many ways, with short, needle-like leaves growing on woody stems and producing clusters of bell-shaped flowers. But this cousin from Southern Africa has rather larger and more delicate flowers, and they come in yellow, pink, purple and white.

French Heather is another of the flowering house plants that are brought into the home for the duration of their flowering season – in this case, from autumn through the earlier part of winter – and then discarded. Pretty though it is, it needs rather special care to keep from year to year, although you could try planting it in the garden in May, in lime-free soil, and bringing it in again in the autumn before it starts flowering again. Since this is not an expensive plant this may, however, not prove sufficiently rewarding.

Erica gracilis is a slightly smaller variety and the one that should, strictly, be called Cape Heath.

Position: Plenty of light, ideally with some direct sunlight during the day.

Temperature: Cool temperatures for preference: between 48°F (8°C) and 65°F (18°C).

Water: Keep the soil moist at all times, but you should use lime-free water or rainwater. Humidity is important: spray daily with lime-free water.

Feeding: Feeding is only necessary if you are keeping the plant from year to year; if so, feed when growing, during the summer.

Propagation: From stem-tip cuttings in late summer.

Soil: Lime-free, peat-based compost.

Problems: The plant will give obvious signs of distress if either too hot and dry or too wet. Prone to common pests.

Euphorbia pulcherrima

'Poinsettia'

It is to the USA that we probably owe the popularity of the Poinsettia: these delightful bushes, with their startling red 'flowers' have now become almost as much a part of the essential Christmas decor as holly and ivy on both sides of the Atlantic, even to the extent that cunningly deceptive artificial Poinsettias are now widely available for those who

despair of keeping the real thing in a healthy state over the Christmas season. In fact this is no longer quite as difficult as it used to be: sensitive though these plants still are, hybrids developed in America are now much better equipped to cope with the fluctuating conditions of the centrally-heated home and it should be quite possible to keep them for at least two months, if

Euphorbia pulcherrima

not six. None the less, there is little point in keeping them after the season is over, unless you have a greenhouse and are prepared to carry out complicated procedures to bring on flowering: like so many of the winter-flowering plants, they are but temporary visitors.

Poinsettias came originally from Mexico, where they

grow as massive bushes up to some 20 ft (6 m) tall; although the house plants that we buy are usually fairly small, they can be anything up to 4 ft (120 cm) tall. The bright red 'flowers' are in fact modified leaves, or bracts, which radiate from the growing tip; the real flowers grow at the centre of these leaves and are comparatively insignificant, like little yellow and green cloves. Another common variety of Poinsettia has white or cream bracts, and there is a hybrid form with a kind of mottled pink and white effect. These are both attractive in their own right, but probably cannot hope to displace the familiar red variety in our affections.

One note of warning: the milky sap of these plants contains poisons and can cause skin irritations.

Position: Plenty of light, ideally with some direct sunlight during the day.

Temperature: Standard room temperatures are fine, so long as they are not allowed to drop below 50°F (10°C) at night.

Water: Keep the soil moist by watering thoroughly and regularly, letting the soil become barely damp before watering again; do not let the soil dry out completely. Poinsettias like humidity, which is best supplied by standing the pot on a base of wet gravel: aerial-spraying may damage the bracts.

Feeding: No feeding is required if the plant is not being kept from year to year.

Propagation: From stem-tip cuttings, but it is very hard to reproduce the compact and colourful plants that are grown commercially.

Soil: Standard peat-based potting compost.

Problems: Leaves dry up and curl: too hot and dry. Drooping and falling leaves: too wet, or too draughty. Prone to common pests.

Fatshedera lizei
'Ivy Tree'

The Ivy Tree deserves its popularity: its glossy, deep-green leaves are elegantly spaced on a woody stem, and if trained up a single support, the plant makes an attractive pillar of foliage which will be quite happy to occupy a fairly shady part of a room. It will grow quickly, and can reach a height of some 10 ft (3 m) over time.

The *Fatshedera lizei* is in fact a hybrid between two different plants within the Araliaceae family: the False Castor Oil Plant (*Aralia japonica* or *Fatsia japonica*) and Ivy (*Hedera helix*). This was one of nature's little accidents that

Fatshedera lizei

took place in a French nursery in 1910: it is, therefore, a comparative newcomer to the house plant world. It has an unusual classification in that, instead of being treated as a variety of either of the parent plants, it has been given its own genus.

The leaves of the Ivy Tree are not abundant, and so three or more are usually planted together. Although a climber, you may have to use some string to give it sufficient purchase on its support. A moss-pole provides the ideal support: not only is it sturdy and sympathetic to look at, but it will also allow the plant to feed through the aerial roots that grow along its stem, provided that you keep the moss damp. To prevent the plant growing taller than you wish, pinch out the growing tip: this will promote side shoots and make the plant look more bushy.

Flowers may appear in late summer: these are similar to

those of the common ivy and look like a compact bunch of greenish-white berries. They are not of great moment, but add a dicreet touch of individuality to a plant more noted for its unflamboyant reliability.

There are variegated forms of the Ivy Tree which incorporate shades of green in the leaf-colouring, or include traces of white, usually at the leaf-margins.

Position: Tolerant of shady poisitions, but actually prefers fairly bright indirect light and even some direct sunlight. Variegated plants will need more light to retain their leaf-markings.
Temperature: Standard room temperatures are fine.
Water: Keep moist; never let the soil dry out, nor on the other hand allow the pot to stand in water.
Feeding: Feed mature plants once a month.
Propagation: From stem-tip cuttings in summer, or by air-layering.
Soil: Standard loam-based potting compost.
Problems: The plant becomes leggy, small leaves: not enough light. Yellowing leaves: too much water. Dry, brown patches on leaves: too hot and dry. Prone to common pests.

Ficus benjamina
'Weeping Fig'

The genus *Ficus* belongs to the Moraceae family, which includes the tree that produces the edible fig, the mulberry tree and the sacred banyan tree of India, as well as a number of popular house plants. The Weeping Fig is one of these; the Rubber Plant is another; and then there is the small, trailing Creeping Fig. They are all so different, both in habit and appearance, that they each deserve a separate section.

The Weeping Fig is an elegant tree with a white trunk

and thin, trailing branches that bear a shower of small, light-green leaves. It looks attractive when small, even at only 2 ft (60 cm) tall, but in the right conditions it can grow indoors to a full-sized tree of some 20 ft (6 m) in height. It

has a happy, light-weight look about it, which, along with its great tolerance of indoor conditions, has made it popular with the designers of large interior spaces, such as shopping malls, where the use of glass canopies can afford sufficient light.

The Weeping Fig is found throughout the warmer parts of the world, but is not a tropical plant and so does not require elaborate protection from our climate. There are a number of varieties available, including a variegated form with touches of cream-white on the leaves.

Ficus benjamina

Position: Plenty of bright indirect light.

Temperature: Standard room temperatures, but winter temperatures must be kept above 55°F (13°C).

Water: Keep moist, but do not allow the plant to stand in water. These plants like humidity and will appreciate aerial-spraying.

Feeding: Feed mature plants once a month from spring to early autumn, when growing.

Propagation: From stem-tip cuttings, or by air-layering; both methods require warmth and humidity.

Soil: Standard loam-based potting compost.

Problems: Leaves turning yellow and dropping: too much water. Leaves withering and drying out: not enough water or humidity. Prone to common pests, particularly scale.

Ficus elastica

'India-rubber Plant' or 'Rubber Plant'

The Rubber Plant was a favourite house plant in Victorian England and has clung steadfastly to its place in the best-sellers' list ever since, even though at times it has shared the same fate as the Aspidistra in being the object of ridicule for no greater reason than its popularity. It is true, you do see Rubber Plants everywhere: but take a fresh look at them and you will see why they have come to be so popular.

The broad, waxy leaves have an almost perfect elliptical shape, finishing at the tip with a soft point. The shiny surface picks out the ribbed contours of the veins, curving away gently at the leaf-margins. There is something wondrous about the finished quality of these leaves, surpassing the workmanship of even the finest polished leather.

Most Rubber Plants are left to grow on a single stem, around which the leaves are distributed with an elegant spaciousness. New leaves will emerge from the growing tip, pushing away the thin, pointed sheath that protects them and unfurling in a fragile, tender green. Older plants will produce side shoots, or side shoots can be encouraged to develop by pinching out the growing tip. (If you do this, be sure to stop the flow of milky sap by applying petroleum jelly or powdered charcoal, or a piece of paper handkerchief.) Somehow, however, the Rubber Plant it at its best when it is a single stem of modest height.

Despite its origins in the warm and wet parts of India, the Rubber Plant is not difficult to grow and will tolerate poor light; but dust and neglect will create out of it a mere ghost of its potential glory. If you really want to be kind to your Rubber Plant, clean the leaves regularly with a damp sponge so that the pores in the leaves do not become clogged up with dust; the kind of polish known as leaf-shine can also be applied once in a while, which will show the leaves off at their best and help to prevent dust from clinging.

There are two main varieties of Rubber Plant: *Ficus elastica* 'Decora' and *Ficus elastica* 'Robusta', both very similar, except that 'Robusta' has wider leaves which grow in a more compact manner. There are also variegated forms of these, with cream or pink splashes on the leaves: these will need rather better light than the all-green varieties.

Another member of the fig family, and similar to the Rubber Plant, is the *Ficus lyrata* (or *Ficus pandurata*), known as the Fiddleleaf Fig. In place of the Rubber Plant's smooth, oval leaves this plant has wide, crinkly leaves, heavily contoured with veins, on very short stalks, and shaped in a form that has clearly reminded someone with a bit of imagination of violins.

Position: Fairly shady positions are acceptable, but bright indirect light promotes better growth and shows the polished quality of the plant to best advantage.
Temperature: Standard room temperatures will keep the plant alive, but a temperature of less that 60°F (16°C) in winter will cause the lower leaves to drop and will inhibit growth.
Water: Keep well watered while the plant is growing in spring and summer; water only occasionally in winter, but keep an eye out for distress (the leaves will droop if thirsty).
Feeding: Feed once a fortnight in summer.
Propagation: By air-layering, or from stem-tip cuttings.
Soil: Standard potting compost.
Problems: Yellowing leaves: too much water or standing in a draught. Drooping leaves: too dry. New leaves have contorted shapes: needs repotting or feeding. Prone to common pests, particularly scale.

Ficus pumila
'Creeping Fig'

This diminutive member of the fig family is not a hugely spectacular plant, but rewarding in its own modest way, and is frequently combined with other plants in assorted pots. Its small, mid-green leaves look like delicate triangles with rounded corners; they bunch together closely to form a compact mat. The long stems are fairly rigid, which prevents the plant from becoming droopy, but they will readily climb up a support if encouraged to do so.

The Creeping Fig is happy to grow away from the light, and will tolerate fairly cold surroundings, but it must have plenty of moisture and humidity, which are presumably abundant in its native habitat in China and Japan. Without permanent moisture it will die.

There is a variegated form which introduces irregular splashes of cream to the leaves: this will require more light than the all-green variety.

Position: Shady positions are perfectly acceptable to the standard variety. Variegated plants require better, but still indirect light.

Temperature: Standard room temperatures are fine; winter temperatures should not be allowed to drop below 45°F (7°C).

Water: Keep moist at all times, but do not allow the pot to stand in water.

Feeding: Feed once a month from spring to summer.

Propagation: From stem-tip cuttings in spring; requires warmth and humidity.

Soil: Either a standard loam-based or a peat-based potting compost.

Problems: Leaves become dry and turn brown: water immediately – it may be too late! Prone to common pests, especially scale.

Gynura sarmentosa

'Velvet Plant' or 'Purple Passion Vine'

This is a plant that might pass almost unnoticed until one day the light catches it from a certain angle and suddenly it is tranformed into an object of fascination. For the charm of the Velvet Plant is the extraordinary texture that is created by the millions of tiny hairs that cover its leaves. These hairs are purple and the leaves are green: when viewed flat on, the greenness of the leaves predominates, but leaves seen from the side have a haze of purple colouring that intensifies according to the angle of view and the curves of the foliage.

The shape of the Velvet Plant is something like that of the common nettle, although its weak stems do allow it to train and thus make it a good candidate for the hanging basket. It is grown exclusively for its foliage: its tiny orange flowers are not very welcome, partly because they have a rather unpleasant smell, but also because they indicate that the plant is getting ready to complete its life-cycle and if they are not pinched out when they appear, the plant will consider its life's work done. Pinch out the growing tips to make a more bushy plant: even if you do this, however, after a couple of years the plant will become straggly and it is then probably best to propagate new plants from stem-tip cuttings and discard the old one.

Velvet Plants are not difficult to grow, but they do need plenty of light and reasonably warm conditions, and they are happier with a little humidity. In other words, the more you can do to emulate the conditions of India and the Far East, from where these plants originate, the happier they will be.

Position: As much light as possible – for the sake of the plant's health, but also so its velvety texture can be seen to best advantage.

Temperature: Normal room temperatures are fine, providing that they do not fall below 60°F (16°C) in winter.

Water: Plenty of water in summer, reducing it in winter so that the soil remains just moist. Results will be improved by standing the pot on a base of wet gravel to provide humidity.

Feeding: Feed with a mild solution of plant food once a month between spring and summer.

Propagation: From stem-tip cuttings, rooted in water before potting.

Soil: Standard loam-based potting compost.

Problems: Leaves losing their purple effect: not enough light. Prone to common pests, particularly aphids.

Hedera

'Ivy'

This is one of our toughest and most enduring house plants – not surprising, perhaps, considering that it is one of the few house plants that is native to our shores and so has a built-in means of surviving our climate. What is unusual is that it can survive quite happily both out of doors and in, and in the range of conditions that this implies. It is also a rare plant that actually seems to want to live indoors, as anyone with a rustic garden shed or garage will probably affirm.

We are all familiar with ivy, with its half-star shaped leaves tumbling down on curvaceous, woody stems. The standard wild species is the *Hedera helix*, and there are numerous varieties of this that are grown as house plants, the only difference between them being the size, coloration and precise shape of the leaves. Most of the common forms are variegated, introducing a number of greens as well as cream, white and pink to the leaf-markings. Others improvise on the standard leaf-shape, such as *Hedera helix*

'Sagittaefolia', or Needlepoint Ivy, which has almost T-shaped leaves, or *Hedera helix* 'Cristata', which is aptly named the Parsley Ivy for its frilly-edged leaves.

There is also another species called *Hedera canariensis*, the Canary Island Ivy, which usually has larger leaves and is almost always found in a variegated form. As its name suggests, it comes from a warmer part of the world and so is not as hardy as *Hedera helix*.

Ivies are happy to trail, and so are good plants to place on shelves or windowsills, or in hanging baskets; they can be encouraged to become more bushy by pinching out the growing tips. They will also climb if given some support. All ivies have aerial roots growing along their stems which are designed to grip to supports, as well as to take up moisture and nutrients in the same way as the roots in the soil. Many ivies grown as house plants, however, have lost the use of these aerial roots through generations of redundancy, and so they may need the help of string to climb effectively.

Position: *Hedera helix* will tolerate extremely shady positions without fuss, but to grow well it really needs bright indirect sunlight; this applies particularly to the variegated ivies. *Hedera canariensis* must have good light to thrive.

Temperature: Standard room temperatures are fine, although none of the ivies like the hot, dry conditions created by central heating.

Water: The soil should be just moist, and can be allowed to dry out between waterings. Supply humidity by daily aerial-spraying when the atmosphere is hot and dry.

Feeding: Feed mature plants once every three months when growing.

Propagation: From stem-tip cuttings rooted in water before potting.

Soil: Standard potting compost.

Problems: Leaves become dry and brown: needs more

moisture and humidity. Leaves marked with dark brown patches: overwatering. Prone to common pests, particularly scale.

Heptapleurum arboricola
'Parasol Plant'

Umbrella imagery seems to have been something of an obsession with the plant-namers: in this case the allusion is hardly apt, unless the inspiration is a Robinson Crusoe-style parasol – after a typhoon. But you can see what they were getting at: the tongue-shaped leaves radiate on gently-arching stalks from the tips of the long stems, giving this plant one of the most elegant and distinctive foliages of all the house plants. This plant will grow to some 4 ft (120 cm) tall, an airy bush of stately, deep-green silhouettes, happy enough to fill a shady corner of a room where other plants would pine away.

Heptapleurum arboricola also has a variegated form, which requires rather more light to maintain its colourings, although prolonged exposure to artificial

Heptapleurum arboricola

light (for example, from a neighbouring table lamp) may suffice. There is also another, similiar species, somewhat larger and rather less dainty called the *Heptapleurum actinophylla* or *Schleffera actinophylla*, or even *Brassaia actinophylla*, which has the common name of – wait for it – the Umbrella Tree. Both the Umbrella Tree and the Parasol Plant are natives of Australasia.

The number of leaves on each stem will vary from four to eight (strictly speaking, these should be called leaflets, and the group of leaflets comprises the leaf). The reason for this is that the younger the plant the fewer (and indeed smaller) the leaflets on each stem. As a result, these plants can often look top-heavy as the older, larger and more heavily populated leaves develop.

Position: Will tolerate fairly shady conditions, but may become straggly as it reaches towards the light; clearly, bright indirect light is best, but avoid direct sunlight.
Temperature: Standard room temperatures are fine, but take care that the temperature does not drop below 55°F (13°C) in winter.
Water: Water thoroughly and regularly, allowing the soil to dry to just damp before each watering.
Feeding: Feed with a mild dose of plant food once a month during the summer.
Propagation: From seed, kept warm in a propagator.
Soil: Standard loam-based potting compost.
Problems: Leaflets turn yellow: too much water, or needs feeding. Plant becomes straggly: needs more light. Prone to common pests.

Hibiscus rosa-sinensis
'Hibiscus' or 'Chinese Rose'

The Hibiscus is a delightful flowering plant, with holly-green leaves and exceptionally lovely flowers: they look like the open 'bell' of a trumpet, out of which protrudes a long spike with a brush of pollen-bearing hairs at its tip.

The house-plant variety of Hibiscus came originally from China, as its alternative common name suggests. There are a number of varieties from all over the tropical world, where they grow in glorious profusion. As house plants, however, they are probably the cause of as much disappointment as joy, for even during the main flowering season from spring to late summer the flowers will only live for a day or two, before rolling back up into a spiral and dropping off – or worse, dropping off when still in bud.

Humidity can bring some alleviation to this problem, but indoor Hibiscus plants really have to be enjoyed for their moments of great pleasure when the flowers do succeed, rather than for a prospect of perpetual flowering. Still the odds improve the older and larger the plant – and Hibiscus plants can last many years and reach up to 4 ft (120 cm) in height if carefully pruned and tended to. It is some compensation, anyhow, that the foliage is attractive in its own right, and evergreen. In the mean

Hisbiscus rosa-sinensis

time, new hybrids are becoming available with single and double flowers in not just the usual red but also yellow, white and orange, and some of these have been bred with a rather better tolerance of indoor conditions than their predecessors.

Position: Plenty of light, with some direct sunlight during the day.

Temperature: As warm as possible, and certainly not lower than 60°F (16°C) at any time.

Water: Keep the soil moist throughout the year, but never let the pot stand in water. Supply humidity by aerial-spraying when budding during the summer, using rain-water if possible.

Feeding: Once a month during the growing season.

Propagation: From stem-tip cuttings in late spring, rooted in water.

Soil: Standard loam-based compost.

Problems: Buds fall off before flowering: too cold, or not enough humidity; keep the temperatures more constant and do not move the plant about. Falling leaves: too much water, or too cold. Prone to common pests, particularly aphids and red spider mite.

Howea forsteriana
'Kentia Palm' or 'Paradise Palm'

Of all the indoor palms, the Kentia Palm is probably the easiest to grow – a fact well appreciated in Victorian and Edwardian Britain where the great hotels featured palm

Howea forsteriana

courts which relied heavily on the effectiveness and tolerance of this plant. Its long, fan-like fronds make an exuberant display of deep, bottle-green foliage which in maturity will reach up to a height of some 8 ft (2.5 m). If you have just acquired a small version, however, do not start moving the furniture yet: they grow very slowly, about 6 in (15 cm) a year, and hence mature palms are very expensive.

The Kentia Palm comes only from the tiny Lord Howe Island; with 6 square miles (15 sq km), a population of 300 and a temperate climate, it lies half way between Australia and New Zealand, and is administered by Australia. Apart from tourism, the production of Kentia-palm seeds is the island's only income-earning industry. This background has given rise to the Kentia palm's Latin name, although it is frequently also referred to as *Kentia forsteriana*.

As single plants Kentia Palms have a rather spindly and famished look, so they tend to be potted up in groups of as many as six at a time to give them the more familiar bushy appearance.

Position: Good light will promote faster growth, but this plant will survive in quite dark positions.

Temperature: Normal room temperatures are fine, although a winter minimum of 50°F (10°C) must be maintained, and at least 60°F (16°C) would be preferable.

Water: Water just enough to keep the soil moist at all times and provide humidity by regular aerial-spraying when conditions are hot and dry. Use lime-free water or rainwater if possible.

Feeding: Feed plants of more than six months old with plant food once a month from spring to autumn only.

Propagation: From seed in a propagator; not easy.

Soil: Standard peat-based compost.

Problems: Fronds drying out and turning brown: atmosphere too hot and dry. Rotting at the base of the plant: soil is waterlogged. Prone to common pests.

Hoya carnosa

'Hoya' or 'Wax Flower'

The Hoya is a plant with its own quite distinctive characteristics and appeal. A climbing or trailing plant with tough, woody stems and thick, fleshy leaves, it is grown for its extraordinary, waxy flowers, which form in disc-like clusters of up to twenty. The individual flowers are no bigger than a drawing-pin head, star-shaped and usually a pink, fleshy colour. They are perhaps not so much beautiful as fascinating for their most unusual texture, but they do also have a heady fragrance – sweet, rich, and slightly musty and cloying. The flowers grow from May to September, developing from the most unpromising-looking, club-like shoots: even greater, therefore, is the wonder of their transformation.

The Hoya is one of those plants that calls out for a shape on which to grow: it is often trained around a hoop, like

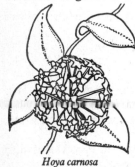

Jasmine. A wire coat-hanger can provide this function perfectly: bend it into an even, oval shape and straighten out the hook so that it can be pushed into the soil as the anchor. Alternatively, find a high position for the plant and let it trail.

There is a variegated form of *Hoya carnosa*, but it does not flower. Other species are available, the most common of which

Hoya carnosa

is *Hoya bella*. This has rather more developed trailing instincts than *Hoya carnosa*, smaller leaves and clusters of superb, snow-white flowers with pink centres. While it is undoubtedly the more beautiful plant, it is also rather more difficult to grow than the more tolerant *Hoya carnosa*.

The Hoya comes from the Far East and tropical Australia. The name may sound exotic, but it in fact refers to a British gardener called Thomas Hoy, who was head-gardener at Syon House, near London, in the late eighteenth century.

Position: Bright indirect sunlight, ideally with some direct sunlight during the day.

Temperature: Standard room temperatures are fine. *Hoya carnosa* will survive winter temperatures of only a few degrees above freezing, but will be happier if kept above 50°F (10°C); *Hoya bella* needs to be kept above 60°F (16°C).

Water: Water well during the flowering season, but allow the soil to dry to barely damp between waterings. Humidity is appreciated, and best supplied by standing the pot on a base of wet gravel.

Feeding: Feed once every other month during spring and summer.

Propagation: From stem-tip cuttings rooted in water; or by air-layering.

Soil: Use a very open, well-drained potting medium containing loam, peat and pea shingle in equal quantities.

Problems: Buds fall before flowering: either the plant has been moved, or it has not received the right amount of moisture. Leaves turning yellowish-brown: too much water.

Hypoestes sanguinolenta
'Freckle Face' or 'Polka Dot Plant'

This is one of the most delightful of the small foliage house plants, as the affectionate common names suggest. The deep green of the leaves, no larger than 2 in (5 cm) in length, is offset by a mass of tiny pink dots, as though the plant has been placed beneath the ladder of an over-vigorous house-painter. In some varieties the dots form larger patterns of colour, even to the extent of making the leaves predominantly pink.

This plant is usually grown as a compact bush of no more than 1 ft (30 cm) high, and is encouraged to take this shape by pinching out the growing tips so that its energies are directed into side shoots. Even after a year or two of careful tending, however, it is likely to become straggly and may best be replaced by young plants propagated from stem-tip cuttings. Given that the Freckle Face started out in the humid warmth of Madagascar, it is not surprising that it still needs some of these conditions to do well in our homes, but it has already gone through several stages of adaptation since the time that it was first introduced in the late nineteenth century as a plant suitable only for the hot-house.

Position: Bright indirect light, without which it will start to revert to green.

Temperature: Keep warm, ideally above 65°F (18°C) throughout the year.

Water: Plenty of water when growing during the summer, easing off in the winter, but keep the soil moist throughout the year. Humidity is best provided by standing the pot on a base of wet gravel.

Feeding: Not required, unless a mature plant is in very tired soil, in which case feed with a mild dose of plant food once a month during the summer, or repot.

Propagation: From stem-tip cuttings (requires warmth and humidity); or from seed.

Soil: Standard peat-based compost.

Problems: Straggly plant with poor colour: not enough light; pinch out growing tips to promote bushiness. Leaves drooping and falling: too cold, too much water. Prone to common pests, especially scale.

Impatiens wallerana

'Busy Lizzie'

Busy Lizzie is a joyous plant with an apt name – although a common name in the USA is Patient Lucy, so it seems that two views are possible. Although there are numerous varieties, they all share a more-or-less similar leaf-shape and all have fleshy, succulent stems which are fragile and need to be handled carefully. The flowers grow at the tips of the stems, from the hub around which the leaves at the stem tip radiate; they are usually red, but may also be orange, purple, pink or white, or even 'candy-striped', and can be single or double.

There are numerous varieties and hybrids on the market

these days, usually derived from the main species, *Impatiens holstii* and *Impatiens sultani*, which are frequently grouped together under the single title *Impatiens wallerana*. These ring the changes not only to the shape and colour of the flowers, but also to the leaves. Some have variegated leaves, mixing white or cream with the green; some have leaves that are a deep purple-green or bronze, notably *Impatiens petersiana*.

With care a Busy Lizzie can be encouraged to flower throughout the year. Plenty of light is the key, and sufficient warmth to trick it into feeling that it is not so far from its rather warmer homelands in Africa, Asia and the Far East. There is a tendency for Busy Lizzies to become leggy, but if you pinch out the growing tips you will encourage side shoots, which will keep the plants bushy; the cuttings can be used for propagation at any time of the year.

Position: Plenty of light, even direct sunlight, but you must be careful not to let the sun scorch the plant through glass.

Temperature: Normal room temperatures should be fine, although the plant will not be happy at temperatures above 70°F (21°C) or below 55°F (13°C).

Water: Water well in the summer when growing and when in flower, less in the winter when the soil should be kept just damp.

Feeding: Feed once every two weeks during the summer when growing and when in flower.

Propagation: From stem-tip cuttings rooted in water and repotted, or from seed.

Soil: Rich, loam-based potting compost.

Problems: Plant becomes straggly, with few, or no, flowers: too dark. Leaves drop off: too cold. Rotting at the base of the stems: too wet. Prone to common pests, especially whitefly and aphids.

Jasminum polyanthum

'Pink Jasmine' or 'Chinese Jasmine'

Jasmine has one of those intriguing fragrances which is a delight to rediscover at each encounter. Pink Jasmine flowers throughout the winter to the early spring: it is a very pretty plant, with long branches bearing small, deep-green, pointed leaves and clusters of pink buds which develop into delicate, sweet-smelling, white flowers looking like star-shaped fanfare trumpets.

Jasminum polyanthum

Pink Jasmine comes from the temperate zones of China and so prefers cool temperatures. It is happy to go outside in the garden for the summer, and be brought inside for the autumn. A warm and humid atmosphere when it first comes indoors after the summer, such as might be provided by a sun room, will help bring on the flowers.

This plant will climb or trail with great determination, and so should be given a support, or even a trellis. Plants sold in the shops are usually entwined around hoops, which display the foliage and flowers to their best advantage. To keep the plant to the shape and size you require, prune it after the flowering season has finished.

There are numerous other species of Jasmine, which flower in different shades and at various times of the year, so if you are addicted to the scent you need never be without it. The most widely known species beside Pink Jasmine is White Jasmine, *Jasminum officinale*, which flowers from early summer to the autumn and is hardy enough to be grown outdoors in places where the winters are not too severe.

Position: Plenty of light, ideally with some direct sunlight during the day.

Temperature: Normal room temperatures are generally fine, except that in winter Jasmines do prefer to be on the cool side: around 55°F (13°C) is ideal; higher temperatures up to 72°F (22°C) are acceptable, but may well inhibit flowering.

Water: Water well at all times, especially when flowering, but do not let the pot stand in water. Provide humidity in hot, dry conditions by daily aerial-spraying, but avoid the flowers if you notice that the spray causes blemishes.

Feeding: Once every two weeks during periods of growth and flowering.

Propagation: From stem-tip cuttings in spring; requires warmth and humidity.

Soil: Standard loam-based potting compost.

Problems: Flowers failing to open: usually caused by lack of light or conditions that are too hot and dry. Prone to common pests.

Kalanchoë blossfeldiana

'Kalanchoë' or 'Flaming Katy'

Flaming Katy seems a rather exaggerated title for this modest plant – it would be more appropriate to think of embers, perhaps; furthermore, these days Kalanchoë flowers can be pink, yellow, orange or white in addition to the original deep red.

Kalanchoë is a succulent that came originally from Madagascar. It has thick, fleshy leaves that bunch up into an irregular, bushy shape no more than about 6 in (15 cm) high and wide; long stems project from the top of this, bearing clusters of tiny flowers.

These are popular plants around Christmas time, when they reach the shops already in flower; they are not expensive and the flowers will bring a touch of colour to the house for several months, if not subjected to the ravages of central heating. At the end of the season they are usually discarded, although by removing the flowers and their stems after the flowering season is over new growth can be encouraged which can then be used as cuttings to produce plants for the following year. To make such plants flower over Christmas, they have to be starved of light for six weeks or so in early autumn, allowing them only eight hours of light a day for this period.

Position: Plenty of light, including direct sunlight when flowering, if possible.

Temperature: Normal room temperatures are fine; in winter keep plants above 50°F (10°C) and below 70°F (21°C).

Water: Water thoroughly at intervals of up to two weeks, ensuring that the pot drains well; allow the soil to become almost dry between waterings. These plants retain moisture in their leaves and suffer if overwatered, inviting rot.

Feeding: Feed once every two weeks when growing and flowering.

Propagation: From seed or from stem-tip cuttings in spring; requires warmth and humidity.

Soil: Standard loam-based potting compost.

Problems: Drooping leaves, signs of rot: too much water.

Maranta leuconeura

'Prayer Plant'

Marantas form one of the most delightful groups of foliage house plants. They all share the same oval-shaped leaves, albeit in different sizes, but the range of leaf-markings within the group is its main fascination. On the one hand, for example, there is *Maranta leuconeura* 'Erythrophylla'(or 'Tricolor'), otherwise known as the Herringbone Plant on account of its extraordinarily precise and vivid leaf-markings, with sharp, red stripes imposed upon the greens of its broad, stiff leaves, which have purple undersides; on the other hand, there is the *Maranta leuconeura* 'Kerchoveana', the true Prayer Plant, with its smaller, softer leaves of grass-green studded with purple-black 'eyes', one of nature's smouldering dark colours. This is also known, rather endearingly, as Rabbit's Foot, for the black markings resemble the tracks of a rabbit. There is also the spectacular *Maranta makoyana* or *Calathea makoyana*, known as the Peacock Plant: the leaves have the texture of satin, grow on long, arching stems and measure up to 1 ft (30 cm) in length; they

Maranta makoyana

have purple undersides and green and white leaf-markings resembling the 'eyes' of a raised peacock's tail. Understandably, it has the alternative common name of Cathedral Windows.

Each of the varieties within the group has something distinctive of this order to offer. This group should, incidentally, include the Calatheas as well as the Marantas. These are in fact two different genera within the Marantaceae family, but they are very similar and the names are frequently used interchangeably.

In their native habitat in Central and South America, Marantas grow on the forest floor, and the smaller species make a thick mat of ground cover. Those with more delicate foliage have found it harder to adapt to the conditions of the living room than their more robust cousins, and so require a fair amount of warmth and humidity.

The name Prayer Plant is said to refer to the way that

these plants raise up their leaves in the evening as the light fades: it seems a happy idea to attribute to this gesture one of meditation at the day's close.

Position: These plants need bright indirect light, but must be protected from strong sunlight or draughts.
Temperature: Marantas prefer warmth; standard room temperatures are fine, provided that they never drop below 50°F (10°C).
Water: Keep the compost moist at all times: neither let the compost dry out completely, nor allow the pot to stand in water. Water less in the winter months. Humidity is vital in hot, dry conditions: supply by aerial-spraying, and if possible place the pot on a base of wet gravel.
Feeding: Feed established plants with a mild dose of plant food once every two weeks during the summer.
Propagation: By root division in spring.
Soil: Standard peat-based compost.
Problems: Dry, brown patches on leaves: too cold, or too dry. Pale leaves: too much sunlight, or needs feeding.

Monstera deliciosa
'Swiss Cheese Plant' or 'Cheese Plant'

This is one of the most popular and widely known of all indoor plants. Hardy enough to withstand a fair amount of neglect, and able to put up with quite shady conditions, it is the sort of plant that you are only too likely to find yourself looking at in the dentist's waiting room or while queuing at the bank.

This should not put you off: the Monstera is a delightful plant with large, forest-green, waxy leaves bearing the deep indentations and holes that have lent it its rather inappropriate association with Swiss *Gruyère* cheese. These indentations (up to ten or so in each leaf on a healthy plant), are thought to be nature's way of reducing the wind resistance of the broad leaves, thus preserving them from the ravages of the fierce winds and hurricanes that play havoc in this plant's native lands, the tropical forests of the Caribbean and Central America.

The Swiss Cheese Plant is not too demanding, but in its native habitat it has space, warmth and humidity, so you should try give it as much of these as you can. It grows slowly – two or three new leaves in a year – but it can live for a very long time in the right conditions and so will need room, for its own comfort but also to be fully appreciated. It is not at all unusual for these plants to grow up to 7 ft (2 m) tall or more.

New leaves, pale and tender, unfurl from the top of the main 'trunk'. The growing tip can be cut off to restrict the plant's growth when there is a danger of it taking over the house. New

Monstera deliciosa

plants can be propagated by cutting off the growing tip beneath the top leaf and placing it in water, or in peaty compost, to root.

The Monstera is a creeping plant rather than a climber and so will usually need to be tied to a stake. It puts out long, woody aerial roots from the main trunk, which go in search of food and water. In the wild these also serve as anchors. Unsightly though they may be, these roots should be respected for the health of the plant, and, if possible, trained into the compost in the plant holder. Alternatively, a moss pole can be used; the roots can be trained around this and, if the moss is watered from time to time, they will be content in performing their proper function.

The Swiss Cheese Plant is also called the Mexican Breadfruit Plant or, in Australia, the Fruit Salad Plant. It may come as a surprise to many Monstera owners to learn that this plant can produce a flower and an edible fruit – although it is unlikely to do so in anything less that perfect conditions, such as a hothouse. This is a member of the Arum (or Araceae) family, and the cream-coloured flowers bear this out; the fruit is like a green cob of maize and has an exotic flavour somewhere between banana and pineapple.

Position: Natural light, but not in direct sunlight. Will tolerate quite shady corners.
Temperature: Warm: winter minimum of 50°F (10°C).
Water: Keep the soil moist, but do not allow the pot to stand in water. Supply humidity by aerial-spraying, or stand the pot on a base of wet gravel.
Feeding: Feed with a mild dose of plant food once a month during the summer.
Propagation: From stem-tip cuttings, stem sections, seeds, or by air-layering.
Soil: Standard peat-based compost.
Problems: Dry, brown patches on the leaves, usually at the tips and borders: too cold, or too much direct sunlight. Yellow leaves: too much water. Prone to common pests, especially scale and red spider mite.

Neanthe bella
'Parlour Palm'

This is another of the palms that are currently staging something of a revival. Although similar in many respects to the Kentia Palm, it has rather coarser leaves, with something of the texture of tough grass; individual stems can produce a healthier number of fronds, but two or three plants are often put in the same pot to give a fuller appearance. The main thing that distinguishes the Parlour

Palm from the Kentia Palm, however, is that the Parlour Palm is much smaller plant, not usually much over 2 ft (60 cm) in height; it is these manageable proportions, no doubt, that have given rise to its common name.

In its Mexican homeland, the Parlour Palm grows in the shade of other trees, and so is happy enough with a shady position in the home, although the less light there is, the slower it will grow – and it is a slow-grower at the best of times. Plants are usually bought when about 1 ft (30 cm) tall and will usually take several years to double in size. Because they are so slow to grow, older and larger plants are expensive to buy.

After about three years the plant may produce a twiggy stem on which tiny yellow flowers grow, followed by small, berry-like fruit – a pretty and unusual effect, like strings of necklace beads when abundant. However, this is unlikely to occur unless the plant receives a fair amount of light.

The Parlour Palm has two Latin names that both seem to have about equal currency: *Neanthe bella* and *Chamaedorea elegans*.

Position: Indirect sunlight; shady conditions are also acceptable.

Temperature: Normal room temperatures are fine, except that in winter this plant prefers to be cool, around 50°F (10°C), and not above 60°F (16°C).

Water: Must be kept moist throughout the year, but do not allow the pot to stand in water.

Feeding: Once every two weeks during the growing period from spring to autumn.

Propagation: From seed; but this requires warmth and humidity and is not easy.

Soil: Standard peat-based compost.

Problems: Fronds drying at the tips and turning brown: too hot and dry. Prone to common pests, particularly red spider mite.

Neoregelia carolinae tricolor
'Cartwheel Plant' or 'Blushing Bromeliad'

This is another house plant from the Bromeliad family, a cousin of the Urn Plant, and likewise deriving its ancestry from the rainforests of South America. It is grown for the impressive, rigid shapes of its leaves which spiral out from the central vase. The lower leaves are variegated, with cream and green stripes running from the base to the tip; and the upper leaves are a rich scarlet.

The Cartwheel Plant produces flowers not unlike those of the Urn Plant, except in this case they never rise up out of the vase. This has inspired an alternative Latin name *Nidularium*, derived from the Latin word meaning 'small bird's nest'. As with almost all Bromeliads, the plant will fade away when flowering is over, but by this time it will have produced little plants, or offsets, around its base which can be repotted to provide new plants.

There are a number of varieties of Neoregelias and Nidulariums, each exhibiting similar traits. Because their attraction tends to be the startling coloration of their rosettes, they should be displayed so that they can be seen from above. They will also need a fair amount of room as they can have a diameter of some 18 in (45 cm), and the tiny teeth that adorn the edges of the leaves of many of the varieties are not too comfortable to live with at close quarters.

Position: Bright indirect light is best.
Temperature: Standard room temperatures are fine, but should not be allowed to drop below 55°F (13°C) in winter.
Water: Keep the central vase filled with water throughout the year; in summer, water the compost as well, but this is not necessary during the winter. In hot, dry conditions, supply humidity by aerial-spraying.

Feeding: Once a month in summer, add a very mild dose of plant food to the water supplied to the central vase.

Propagation: From offsets produced by the mother plant after flowering, but wait until they are a reasonable size; preferably in spring.

Soil: A mixture of standard peat-based and loam-based potting composts in equal parts.

Problems: Leaves droop and dry out: no water in the central vase. Rot: overwatering. Prone to common pests, in particular scale and mealy bug.

Nephrolepsis exaltata

'Ladder Fern' or 'Sword Fern'

This is the fern we have all seen and which most of us would love to keep: broad fronds of wavy leaves cascade forth in elongated triangles, producing a dense clump of vibrant green – when the plant is healthy. But so often this plant quietly wilts, leaving us with little more than handfuls of bone-dry leaves to tidy away, and the forlorn, denuded stems.

What this plant absolutely must have is humidity, and then it must have plant food when it is growing and space to grow into. Without this attention all its promise will be lost. The Victorians loved this plant, and one can only surmise that it did well for them because it never had to suffer the fatal, dry heat of central heating.

There are a number of species of Ladder Fern. The basic one is *Nephrolepsis exaltata*, which grows naturally in various parts of the tropical world; it is now sold in a number of varieties such as 'Fluffy Ruffles' (the Feather Fern), 'Whitmanii' (the Lace Fern), and 'Bostoniensis' (the Boston Fern), which has been responsible for the widespread success of this plant in the USA. All of these can produce fronds of up to 30 in (75 cm) in length, given the right conditions, making them ideal subjects for hanging baskets. There is also the *Nephrolepsis cordifolia*, which has rather smaller proportions.

Position: Bright indirect light is best, but will tolerate fairly shady conditions. Keep out of draughts.

Temperature: Normal room temperatures are fine, but ideally keep them somewhere between 50°F (10°C) and 70°F (21°C).

Water: Never allow the compost to dry out, nor allow the pot to stand in water; it should be just moist all the time. Spray daily with lime free water, or rainwater, especially in hot, dry, conditions; additional humidity can be supplied by placing the pot on a base of wet gravel.

Feeding: Feed established plants every two weeks during the summer, when growing.

Propagation: From plantlets growing from runners in early summer; or by root-division in the spring.

Soil: Standard peat-based compost.

Problems: Leaves drying up and falling: too dry, lack of humidity.

Pachystachys lutea

'Lollipop Plant' or 'Golden Shrimp Plant'

This plant earns its common names from its tall, upright candles of yellow 'flowers' which are similar in many ways to those of the *Beloperone guttata*, to which it is related, which likewise has its origins in tropical South America, and which, confusingly, is called the Shrimp Plant. It is, however, rather different to the Shrimp Plant and has an altogether more noble aspect.

The leaves are dark green and fairly large, forming a slightly untidy-looking bush out of which rise the flower-heads – a series of yellow, modified leaves (bracts) which overlap like fish-scales to create a tall pyramid. From between the bracts grow the actual flowers themselves: delicate white trumpets, curving downwards.

The Lollipop Plant is often discarded in autumn after its long flowering season, but it is quite possible to keep a plant from year to year by pruning it hard after flowering. However, the foliage is not particularly attractive on its own, and the plant is likely to become leggy after a couple of years, so it may be as well to take stem-tip cuttings each spring to propagate new plants for the coming year.

Pachystachys lutea

Position: Plenty of light, including direct sunlight, especially when flowering.

Temperature: Standard room temperatures are fine, but keep above 50°F (10°C) in winter.

Water: Water regularly to keep the soil moist, but allow the soil to become almost dry before watering again. Provide humidity by standing the pot on a base of wet gravel; aerial-spraying during the flowering season can cause rot.

Feeding: Feed once every three weeks when in flower.

Propagation: From stem-tip cuttings in spring; requires warmth and humidity.

Soil: Standard loam-based potting compost.

Problems: Leaves falling: too dry, or too cold, or waterlogged. Prone to common pests.

Pelargonium

'Pelargonium' or 'Geranium'

Pelargonium is the correct term for this, one of the most popular of the flowering house plants. Geranium is really the term for the hardy outdoor plant of the same family, but has also become a common name for the Pelargonium. These are now produced in a bewildering number of hybrid forms which play on the various possibilities for the colours of the flowers, the composition of the flower-head, the length of the flower-stem, and the colour and variegations of the leaves. The result is that there are now some quite superb varieties available with flowers in pink, white, orange and red, single and double, with leaves of green and purple and cream.

There are two main groups of flowering Pelargoniums, both originating from South Africa. First there are the Zonal Geraniums (*Pelargonium zonale* or *Pelargonium hortorum*), with the characteristic rounded leaves, often marked with rings of colour; these are the common Geraniums that are used as bedding plants and which, with enough light, will flower all year. Then there are the Regal or Martha Washington Geraniums (*Pelargonium domesticum* or *Pelargonium grandiflorum*), which have rather fuller petals to the flowers, and leaves that are more triangular and more heavily contoured and serrated; they only have a limited flowering season (usually late spring and early summer) and are harder to grow than the Zonal Geraniums. In addition to these there are also the delightful Trailing or Ivy-leaved Geraniums (*Pelargonium peltatum*), with their more waxy leaves and large-petalled flowers – perfect for hanging baskets.

Foliage Pelargoniums are becoming increasingly popular. These produce only insignificant flowers, but the leaves of several of the varieties have the delicate lines of tracery and can be massed into impressive bushes of soft, grey-green colour. But their particular charm is their scent. Whereas the flowering Pelargoniums have a rather distinctive, musty smell, the foliage Pelargoniums have the most intriguing, herbal fragrances which are revealed when the leaves are brushed against or crushed between your fingers.

Pelargonium crispum, the Lemon Geranium, has frilly-edged, variegated leaves with a fresh, peppery-lemon scent; *Pelargonium graveolens*, the Rose Geranium, has superb, lace-like leaves and a scent to match its common name. There is also a Mint Geranium, *Pelargonium tomentosum*.

Position: Flowering Pelargoniums should have plenty of light, ideally with some direct sunlight during the day. Foliage Pelargoniums do well in bright indirect sunlight.

Temperature: Standard room temperatures are fine, but Pelargoniums prefer to be kept on the cool side over winter, between 50°F (10°C) and 60°F (16°C) for preference.

Water: Water thoroughly at regular intervals, allowing the soil to become almost dry between waterings. Ease off watering in winter. Pelargoniums do not need humidity.

Feeding: Feed with a mild dose of plant food once a month from spring to autumn (too much fertilizer can inhibit the production of flowers).

Propagation: By stem-tip cuttings in spring or summer; or from seed in spring.

Soil: Standard peat-based or loam-based compost. Repot in the spring but do not put into too large a pot as this will inhibit the production of flowers.

Problems: Leggy growth, few flowers: not enough light. Leaves go yellow and drop off: soil too dry. Rot: over-watering. Prone to common pests, particularly whitefly.

Peperomia

'Peperomia'

The Peperomias come from Central and South America and belong to the same family, the Piperaceae, as the pepper plant (as in salt and pepper). They provide a range of interesting foliage house plants which can be grouped into two main categories: the upright Peperomias and the bushy Peperomias.

The most common of the upright Peperomias is the Desert Privet, *Peperomia magnoliaefolia*, so called because the leaves are said to resemble those of a Magnolia, but its common name is a rather more helpful description. This plant is usually seen in its variegated form, with green, fleshy leaves spotted with yellow flecks. Although the leaves are about four times the size of privet leaves, the resemblance is striking.

The bushy species provide a rather more spectacular range. The leaves are less fleshy than those of the Desert Privet, heart-shaped and usually have highly distinctive markings and textures. *Peperomia argyreia*, for example, has leaves of some 4 in (10 cm) long with a deep-green background and silver-grey markings, like the trailing tentacles of an octopus, which radiate from the point where the stalk joins the leaf. *Peperomia caperata* is plain green in its ordinary form, but with a deeply crinkled surface: the variegated form has a free-hand splash of green in the middle of an otherwise white leaf. They all grow as compact bushes, less than 12 in (25 cm) tall – neat, pleasing and interesting. Some of the varieties add to their virtues by producing extraordinary flower-heads which stand upright above the foliage, like bent incense sticks or rats' tails.

Position: Bright indirect light.
Temperature: Standard room temperatures are fine, but the Peperomias appreciate warmth; winter temperatures must stay above 50°F (10°C).
Water: Keep on the dry side: most Peperomias have fleshy leaves that can store water. Supply humidity by standing the pot on a base of wet gravel, and in summer by aerial-spraying.
Feeding: Feed established plants with a mild dose of plant food once a month during the summer.
Propagation: Upright varieties: from stem-tip cuttings in spring. Bushy varieties: from leaf cuttings.

Soil: Standard loam-based potting compost.
Problems: Leaves dry up and/or leaves drop off: too cold, too dry. Prone to common pests.

Philodendron
'Philodendron'

The Philodendrons are members of the Arum (or Araceae) family, which is the source of a large number of our house plants. They are closely related to the Monsteras and very similar in appearance, especially when young, to the extent that the Swiss Cheese Plant, *Monstera deliciosa*, is sometimes also known as the Splitleaf Philodendron and as such bears the alternative Latin name of *Philodendron pertusum*.

Philodendrons are prodigious climbers, and in their native tropical South America will climb trees to a height of some 60 ft (18 m). Indeed the name 'philodendron' means 'tree-lover' in Greek in acknowledgement of this habit. However, there are also non-climbing Philodendrons, some of which bear little resemblance to the rest of the genus, such as the *Philodendron callinofolium*, with its strap-like leaves growing on a central stem rather like a palm.

Of the climbing Philodendrons the *Philodendron scandens* or Sweetheart Vine is probably the most popular. This has beautiful heart-shaped leaves of moderate size and grows into a luxuriant, bushy pillar, especially when supported on a moss pole, which will provide moisture and nutrients to the aerial roots that grow from the main stem. As with most Philodendrons, it is the shiny, leathery quality of the leaves that is its particular attraction. This is a very tolerant plant and seems so happy in the highly variable atmosphere of bathrooms that it has earned for itself the alternative common name of the Bathroom Plant.

There are numerous other species of Philodendron, each with foliage of differing shapes and markings: some have leaves that are deeply indented or star-shaped, such as the *Philodendron panduriforme*, the Fiddleleaf Philodendron or Panda Plant. The *Phildendron angustisectum* has leaves that are so deeply indented with slashes that they have been reduced to the shape of a rib-cage. Others have solid, triangular leaves, or leaves in the shape of an arrowhead. Colours range of deep green to copper-green tinged with purple, or variegated with white. The leaves are usually glossy and leathery, but some species have leaves that are covered with tiny, velvety hairs, such as the *Philodendron melanochrysum*, the Black Gold Philodendron.

Although grown as foliage plants, Philodendrons do flower; however, only the climbing species are likely to do so in the home. The flowers are not particularly significant, usually all-green versions of the hooded spathe-and-spadix kind of flower typical of the Arum family, like our native Cuckoopint.

Philodendrons are, on the whole, not difficult to keep, and some seem tolerant of even the most shameful neglect. Needless to say, however, providing the right conditions brings out the best in these plants.

Position: Bright indirect light.
Temperature: Moderate warmth, above 55°F (13°C) in winter.
Water: Keep the soil little more than moist throughout the year. Humidity is welcome in hot, dry conditions: supply by aerial-spraying.
Feeding: Feed once a month from spring to autumn.
Propagation: From stem-tip cuttings or stem cuttings; or, with the non-climbing species, from basal shoots. All methods will require warmth and humidity.
Soil: Standard peat-based or loam-based potting compost.
Problems: Yellowing leaves: too much water. Tired, lustreless look: plant needs watering and feeding. Prone to common pests, especially scale.

First aid for ailing house plants

Promptness is the key to curing the various ailments that afflict house plants. If you recognize the symptoms soon enough, most problems will be easy to correct. Even insects are readily dealt with if you discover them before they begin to multiply and spread out of control, attacking one plant after another.

Set up a regular inspection schedule. Begin with the foliage, especially the light-coloured new growth, which quickly shows signs of damage or weakness; the brown spots that come from too low a humidity level or too much

heat generally start out as very tiny specks. Remember to check the undersides of the leaves where insects are most likely to congregate.

Insects are not as great a problem to plants indoors as they are outdoors, but they can be brought into the house on new plants. If insects appear on established plants, place the plants in quarantine to keep pests from spreading. Most insects can be washed off with soapy water or swabbed away with alcohol. Serious infestations require chemicals, but be careful to follow the directions on the labels.

DESCRIPTION	WHAT TO DO
APHIDS Aphids may be green, red, pink, yellow, brown or black. They congregate on soft young tips or the undersides of leaves, and suck out a plant's juices, stunt new growth and cause foliage to die. They secrete honeydew, that becomes a host to sooty black mould.	Pick off and crush any visible aphids, then wash the plant – either dunk it upside down into warm soapy water or swab leaves and stems with a soft soapy cloth. Rinse the foliage with clear tepid water. For serious infestations spray with insecticide.

DESCRIPTION	WHAT TO DO
WHITEFLY Tiny sucking insects that flutter off the leaves when a plant is disturbed. The eggs laid or the undersides of leaves hatch into green larvae that feed on plant sap and do most of the damage. Green leaves turn yellow and drop. Like aphids, they deposit honeydew.	For mild cases, wash the leaves with a strong spray of tepid water, making sure to cleanse the undersides thoroughly. Treat serious attacks with insecticide.
RED SPIDER MITE Sometimes orange-red, this tiny pest is more usually yellow-green in colour. They feed by sucking sap causing the leaves to become mottled and pale green in colour. Spider mites live under leaves, spinning white webs that cover the plant. The plants become stunted and die.	Wash small plants at the sink with a strong spray of tepid water; large plants should be wiped with a soft soapy cloth, then rinsed with tepid clear water. For serious infestations, spray with insecticide.

DESCRIPTION		WHAT TO DO
	SCALE Scale, which congregate on the undersides of leaves along the main veins, look like oval shells about 3mm (⅛in) long, but their yellowish or greenish brown colour makes them hard to see until the infestation is severe. Scales also deposit honeydew.	Gently scrub the scales off the leaves, using warm soapy water and a small brush, then rinse. Treat severely infested plants with insecticide.
	MEALY BUGS The soft 6mm (¼in) long bodies of mealy bugs are coated with white powdery wax; they look like bits of cotton clustered under leaves and in crevices on the tops of leaves that are in shade. By sucking sap, they stunt and kill plants.	Dab with a cotton swab dipped in methylated spirits; they will die and fall off. Then wash the plant with warm soapy water and rinse it with clear water. Spray severely infested plants with insecticide.

DESCRIPTION	WHAT TO DO
Lower leaves of most afflicted plants turn yellow, and stems become soft and dark in colour; cacti become mushy. Soil stays soggy and green scum forms on clay pots. CAUSE Too much water.	Make sure the pot's drainage hole is not clogged and do not let the plant stand in water in its saucer for over half an hour. If the soil has become compacted, roots may decay for lack of oxygen; repot the plant. Water only if necessary. Spray with a foliar feed to hasten recovery.
Leaf edges of most afflicted plants dry and curl under, or lower leaves turn yellow with brown spots and fall; cacti and succulents become yellowed. CAUSE Too little water or too much heat.	Water until the excess runs out of the drainage hole in the bottom of the pot; thereafter water as specified for the plant. If the condition persists, move the plant to a cooler location. Spray with a foliar feed to encourage new root development.

DESCRIPTION		WHAT TO DO
	Yellow or brown patches develop on the leaves of most afflicted plants, or leaves on one side of the plant turn brown; cacti become yellow. CAUSE: Too much light; sunscorch.	Move the plant farther from the window so that it will not be subject to so much direct heat, or shield it with a curtain. If the plant is growing under incandescent lamps, move it farther from the bulbs or use lower-wattage bulbs that generate less heat.
	Stems of most afflicted plants stretch towards the light source and grow very long; leaves on new stems are pale-coloured and small. On cacti, the new growth looks weak. CAUSE: Too little light.	Move the plant closer to a window or to a brighter exposure to get more sunlight. If it is growing under artificial light, shift the plant nearer to the centre of the bulbs, or increase the wattage or number of bulbs used and keep them on longer.

DESCRIPTION	WHAT TO DO
Leaf tips turn brown especially on ferns; leaves or stems appear to be crushed or broken. CAUSE: Bruising.	For appearance' sake, use scissors to cut off the damaged sections of foliage, keeping as much of each leaf or stem intact as possible. Move the plant to a more protected location where people are less likely to brush against it.
New growth is rapid but weak and the plant wilts. A white crust of built-up salts develops on the surface of the soil or on the outside of clay pots. CAUSE: Too much fertilizer.	Give the plant more light. Fertilize less frequently or at half the suggested concentration. If salts have formed, water the plant thoroughly to dissolve them; then water again in half an hour to wash the dissolved salts through the pot's drainage hole. Scrape salts off the pot's rim and sides.

DESCRIPTION		WHAT TO DO
	Leaves fade to a pale green and lower leaves turn yellow and drop off. New leaves are small or growth stops. CAUSE: Too little fertilizer.	Fertilize more often, especially during the plant's growing season.
	Leaves turn yellow and fall off suddenly; the plant tissues appear glassy and translucent. CAUSE: Sudden rise or fall in temperature.	Move the plant away from draughts, air conditioners or radiators. When the damage is severe, remove the plant from the pot. If the roots have rotted, discard the plant; if the roots are healthy, prune them back to keep them in balance with the surviving top growth and repot the plant.

DESCRIPTION		WHAT TO DO
	Leaf edges turn brown, and eventually leaves die and fall off. CAUSE: Too little humidity.	Place the pot on a bed of moist pebbles in a tray or in a larger container with moist moss peat around it or in an enclosed terrarium. Mist the leaves regularly.
	Plant appears crowded; roots protrude from the drainage hole in the bottom of the pot or crop out on top of the soil. Plant wilts between waterings or produces only a few small leaves. CAUSE: Plant is too big for its pot.	Repot the plant in a larger container. Spray with a foliar feed to encourage development of new roots in fresh compost.

Pilea cadierei

'Pilea' or 'Aluminium Plant'

The Pileas provide an agreeable, if unassuming, range of foliage house plants. They form small, bushy mounds of heavily quilted leaves which have colours ranging from greens, variegated with yellow, white or silver, to bronze. *Pilea cadierei* is called the Aluminium Plant because of the metallic colouring of the splodges of variegation which fill the spaces between the veins of its green leaves, but each of the other species in the group exhibit their own individual coloration and leaf-texture.

Pileas come from countries throughout the tropical world and are actually members of the Urticaceae family, which includes the common nettle and the hop used in brewing. Despite their origins, they are remarkably tolerant of living conditions in the average home and are not difficult to grow. To keep a plant compact, the growing tips should be pinched out from time to time; after a couple of years, however, it is likely to become straggly and so it is best to propagate new plants each year to ensure that you have a fine-looking, mature plant at all times.

A rather novel Pilea – and one of the easist to grow – is the *Pilea muscosa*, which was first brought back from tropical South America in the late eighteenth century. Unlike other members of this family, it has fern-like branches of leaves and produces small, yellowish flowers containing abundant pollen. When the plant is tapped the pollen bursts forth like a puff of smoke, which reminded those who first delighted in this phenomenon of the puffs of gunpowder in cannon fire, and so earned the plant its common name, the Artillery Plant.

Position: Bright indirect sunlight.
Temperature: Warmth is preferred; ensure that winter temperatures are above 50°F (10°C).

Water: Water well during the summer, and ease off over winter, making sure that the soil never dries out. Supply humidity when conditions are hot and dry by means of regular aerial-spraying.

Feeding: Feed with a mild dose of plant food once a month during the summer.

Propagation: From stem-tip cuttings in spring.

Soil: Standard loam-based potting compost mixed in equal measure with extra peat.

Problems: If too dry or too wet, the leaves will show their discomfort by drooping. Prone to common pests, especially aphids.

Platycerium bifurcatum

'Staghorn Fern'

This is one of those house plants that is more likely to inspire fascination than admiration for its beauty. The Staghorn Fern has broad, branching leaves, flattened like straps and shaped, as the name suggests, like a deer's horns.

This is a real fern, bearing spores on its upper fronds; it also has bulbous-looking lower fronds which are sterile and turn a papery-brown as the plant matures.

The Staghorn Fern comes from Australia and South East Asia, where it grows as an epiphyte – that is, it grows on other plants or trees without actually feeding off them. As with most epiphytes, its roots function primarily as anchors so require virtually no soil; nutrients are supplied by the plant itself through the gradual degeneration of the sterile fronds. These plants, therefore, are often grown in sphagnum moss wedged into pieces of cork bark. They are also excellent for hanging baskets, since their unusual, trailing shapes are best admired from below.

Platycerium bifurcatum is sometimes also known as

Platycerium alcicorne. Another species, the *Platycerium grande*, the Royal Elkhorn Fern, grows with even wider fronds in an upright, vase-like shape and looks like some kind of giant seaweed growing underwater. It is more tender than the very resilient Staghorn Fern, and needs more care.

Platycerium bifurcatum

Position: Bright indirect sunlight.

Temperature: Warmth is preferred, but *Platycerium bifurcatum* can tolerate temperatures as low as 50°F (10°C) in winter; *Platycerium grande* needs to be kept above 65°F (18°C).

Water: Water regularly by plunging the container or base into water and soaking thoroughly, then draining it well; it should remain moist at all times. Supply humidity by aerial-spraying.

Feeding: Supply a mild dose of plant food once a month.

Propagation: From offsets (young plants) that may grow at the base of the plant; or from spores (not easy).

Soil: Standard peat-based compost; or if grown on bark, chopped sphagnum moss mixed with standard peat-based compost in equal measure.

Problems: Fronds drooping limply: too dry. Upper fronds turning brown at the edges: too cold or too wet. Prone to common pests, especially scale.

Primula

'Primula' or 'Primrose'

Primulas are related to the wild spring Primrose of woodlands and gardens, with its wrinkled leaves and pale-yellow flowers. Somehow indoor Primulas never quite have that pristine freshness of the wild Primrose, but none the less they are attractive, bushy plants and make a fine show of colour.

Primulas are usually treated as flowering annuals, tolerated while they flower and then discarded. However, they do have a long flowering season, usually some four months over winter, from about December through to March. In fact there is nothing to stop you keeping a plant from year to year if you accept its gradually declining output of flowers and the months of resting.

The garden Primrose (*Primula acaulis*) has been adapted for indoor use, as has the Polyanthus (*Primula variabilis*), which flowers in yellow, pink, red, mauve, purple, blue and white, and bicolour combinations of these. Those grown specifically for indoor use include the Fairy Primrose (*Primula malacoides*), with its sprays of small, fragrant flowers in pink, white, mauve and red, and its frilly-edged leaves; the Chinese Primrose (*Primula sinensis*), often with frilly petals and rounded, hairy leaves shaped rather like a Pelargonium's leaves; and the Poison Primrose (*Primula obconica*) with balls of flowers on long stems, so named because the leaves can cause skin rashes.

Position: Bright indirect light.

Temperature: Cool, for preference; winter temperatures should not drop below 40°F (4°C), and should ideally be kept around 50°F (10°C), and a little warmer for *Primula sinensis*.

Water: Keep just moist throughout the year. In hot, dry conditions supply humidity by occasional aerial-spraying (but avoid spraying the flowers), or by placing the pot on a base of wet gravel.

Feeding: Feed once every two weeks when flowering.

Propagation: From seed in summer, in cool conditions; or by division after flowering.

Soil: Standard peat-based compost.

Problems: Leaves dry out at the edges: too hot and dry. Short flowering season: too hot. Prone to common pests, especially whitefly and red spider mite.

Pteris cretica

'Table Fern' or 'Ribbon Fern'

The Pteris ferns form an interesting group; if rather less spectacular than Nephrolepsis ferns, they have their quiet charms with their crinkly leaves and less crowded stems. The most popular is probably the *Pteris cretica* 'Alexandrae', the Cristate Table Fern, with its irregularly serrated fronds, like flaming swords, and curious cockscomb tips.

Most Table Ferns never grow very large: the fronds reach a maximum of about 12 in (30 cm). The *Pteris tremula*, or Australian Brake Fern, will, however, grow up to 4 ft (120 cm) tall and has elegant, spindly fronds on long stalks which look like the leaves of some kind of undernourished giant carrot.

There are two variegated Pteris ferns, which make a welcome change to the standard green. There is the *Pteris cretica* 'Variegata', which is just the variegated form of the standard Table Fern; and then there is the small *Pteris ensiformis* 'Victoriae', known as

Pteris cretica 'Alexandrae'

the Silver Fern on account of the silver strips along the central veins of the leaflets that make up the triangular-shaped fronds.

These ferns come from temperate and tropical countries around the world, particularly Australia. They are not difficult to grow and tolerate the hot, dry air of centrally-heated homes rather better than than most of the other, more delicate ferns.

Position: Shady position, weak indirect light.
Temperature: Standard room temperatures are fine, as long as they stay above 50°F (10°C) in the winter.
Water: Keep the compost moist throughout the year: never allow it to dry out. Supply humidity by aerial-spraying, or by standing the pot on a base of wet gravel.
Feeding: Feed once a month during the summer with a mild dose of plant food.
Propagation: By root division; or by sowing spores in spring (not easy).
Soil: Standard peat-based potting compost.
Problems: Fronds dry up and turn brown: too hot and dry. Fronds turn pale: too much light.

Saintpaulia ionantha
'African Violet'

The African Violet is surely one of the most endearing of the flowering house plants. The original variety comes from Southern Africa and is named after its discoverer, Baron Walter von St Paul; it has deep blue clusters of flowers on long, branching stems. These flowers have a very delicate, crystalline glow to them – rather like sugared violets – and large, yellow stamens at the centre. The deep-green leaves are stiff, but form gentle, rounded folds, heavily contoured and usually coated in delicate hairs that give them a soft, velvety sheen (although there are some varieties with smooth leaves).

There are now numerous other varieties and hybrids available, in various different colours, sizes and petal-shapes: white, pink, light blue, mauve, lilac, deep purple and bicolours; single, double, frilled; standard, large and dwarf.

African violets are not at all difficult to grow successfully and will flower almost the whole year long, given the correct amount of light and level of warmth. The real secret is to water the plant at the base of the pot only, and to make sure it is not left to stand in excess water: water should not be allowed to touch the leaves, which are highly susceptible to mould. Simple, but advice that is too freqently ignored, with sad results. The plant will be happier, and will flower better in summer, if you allow it to rest for a couple of months in a lower temperature

Saintpaulia ionantha

(about 55°F or 13°C) during the late winter, easing up on watering so that the soil is kept just moist.

The African Violet, incidentally, belongs to the Gesneriaceae family and is no relation of the familiar garden violet, *Viola odorata*.

Position: Bright indirect light.

Temperature: Best kept at around 60°F (16°C), i.e. below normal central-heating warmth. Ensure that winter temperatures do not drop below 50°F (10°C).

Water: Use tepid water supplied to the base of the pot only; keep the soil damp at all times, but make sure that the plant does not sit in water. African Violets like humidity; provide this by placing the pot on a base of wet gravel, not by aerial-spraying.

Feeding: Feed with a mild dose of plant food when the plant is growing during the summer.

Propagation: From seed in spring; or from leaf cuttings pinned to the soil; or from leaf-and-stem cuttings in soil. Each of these methods requires warmth and humidity.

Soil: Standard peat-based compost.

Problems: Flowers and leaves look unhealthy and develop spotting: too cold and wet, or water has been poured on to the leaves, or the plant has been scorched by direct sunlight. Buds fail to develop: too hot and dry, or insufficient light. Prone to common pests, especially white-fly and mealy bug.

Sansevieria trifasciata
'Mother-in-law's Tongue' or 'Snake Plant'

It may be the popularity of this plant that accounts for the vehemence of opinions about it: some people love its extraordinary shape, with its sword-like leaves standing tall and bolt-upright, quite unlike any other house plant; others absolutely detest it. Certainly too many of them on a windowsill do create a rather austere, forbidding impression. Or is it the unflattering common names that suggest to

Sansevieria trifasciata

people that they should think ill of the plant? Whoever branded the poor Sansevieria with the name Mother-in-law's Tongue may have been a wit, but certainly was no admirer.

Sansevieria trifasciata has dark-green leaves striped with ripples of silvery green. We are more likely to come across the variety called 'Laurentii', which has cream-coloured borders running the length of the leaves. Both sorts can grow up to 3 ft (90 cm) high, although they are more usually about half this height; in any case, make sure that your pot has a wide-enough base to prevent the plant toppling over when fully grown.

Sansevieria trifasciata will sometimes flower, producing a spike bearing curly little yellow-green flowers, a bit like a wild Bluebell in its shape. This should be cut back when the flowers die away.

The Sansevierias come from West Africa and are named after an eighteenth-century Italian prince, Raimondo di Sangro of San Severo, in northern Apulia. Another species is grown as a house plant: *Sansevieria hahnii*. This has a rather more squat form, and grows around a central rosette.

These are all extremely easy plants to grow. They need precious little pampering and will remain perfectly happy on the sole condition that they are never swamped with water.

Position: Not fussy: either sunlight, or shade, even weak indirect light.

Temperature: Standard room temperatures are fine; winter minimum of 50°F (10°C).

Water: Water regularly, giving the plant plenty of water in the summer but allowing the soil to dry out between waterings. In winter keep the soil barely moist; too much water over the winter can cause rotting at the base of the stems.

Feeding: Feed established plants once a month in summer.

Propagation: From leaf cuttings (requires warmth); variegated plants, however, will revert to green if propagated by this method. To avoid this, propagate by dividing the rhizome (undergound stem) and repotting the plantlets that grow from it.

Soil: Standard loam-based potting compost.

Problems: Almost all problems stem from overwatering: brown spots on the leaves, rot etc. The leaves will wilt if the plant is not receiving enough water. Prone to common pests, especially mealy bug.

Saxifraga sarmentosa
'Mother of Thousands'

This is a charming, compact plant with round, silver-veined leaves of deep green, softened by a coating of tiny hairs. Its main characteristic is the trail of long runners that hang down from it, at the end of each of which dangle young plantlets. This explains the plant's most usual common name, as well as a host of others that it has acquired: Roving Sailor, Magic Carpet, Aaron's Beard (which 'went down to the skirts of his garments', *Psalms* 133), and Strawberry Geranium (after the similar manner in which strawberries reproduce, and the fact that the leaves resemble those of a Geranium).

The runners, which are at their most active during the summer months, can reach to over 1 ft (30 cm) in length, making this a fascinating subject for a hanging basket. But these are not this plant's only attractions: it also flowers. During the summer flower-spikes will rise above the foliage and produce clusters of pretty little flowers with white petals and pink and yellow centres.

After a couple of years a Mother of Thousands will start to look rather ragged. Who can blame her? She has worked valiantly to ensure the continuation of her kind, and one can make advantage of her endeavours by propagating new plants from the plantlets to replace the mother on her retirement.

The Mother of Thousands came from China originally, where it was used to a temperate climate; it prefers, therefore, to stay on the cool side in the home. It has an alternative Latin name, *Saxifraga stolonifera*. There is also a variegated form which is called 'Tricolor' for its green, cream and pink leaves. This is more tender than the standard variety, and so needs to be kept in slightly more warmth and light.

Position: Plenty of indirect sunlight.

Temperature: Standard room temperatures are fine, and can drop as low as 40°F (4°C) in winter. Avoid exposing the plant to temperatures above 65°F (18°C).

Water: Water well in summer, when growing; if the plant does suffer a drought it usually revives well.

Feeding: Feed once every three months from spring to late summer.

Propagation: Place the plantlets directly into soil. For best results, wait until the plantlet has rooted before cutting the runner that attaches it to the mother plant.

Soil: Standard loam-based potting compost.

Problems: This plant will only suffer if severely over-watered or underwatered: symptoms of distress will be obvious. Prone to common pests, especially aphids.

Scindapsus aureus

'Devil's Ivy' or 'Golden Pothos'

This is another member of the Arum (or Araceae) family and similar in leaf-shape and colouring to its relatives the Chinese Evergreen (*Aglaonema trewbii*) and the Dumb Cane (*Dieffenbachia picta*). Devil's Ivy is an elegant climbing plant with broad, variegated leaves that arch away from the main stems on long stalks. New leaves grow from the tip of the stems, first appearing as tightly spiralled spikes which then unfurl in a tender green.

A mature Devil's Ivy can grow to a considerable length, anything up to 15 ft (4·5 m). As its gets older and larger, so the leaves become bigger: thus a small plant will have leaves of only some 4 in (10 cm) in length, whereas a mature plant can have leaves at least twice this size. In their native Solomon Islands in the South Pacific, the leaves can be as much as 2 ft (60 cm) long.

Devil's Ivy does not miss the warmth and humidity of the

South Pacific as much as one might expect: temperatures have to be kept above a certain minimum, but otherwise normal room temperatures suffice. However, balancing the correct amount of water and light is not easy, and only too often leaves will develop brown spots and go yellow. To maintain the growth of a young plant, repot in spring. At a certain point it will begin to need supporting; a moss pole is ideal for this, as the damp moss inside it will provide moisture and nutrients to the aerial roots, and this in turn will help to induce the plant to produce larger leaves. Alternatively, the plant can be allowed to trail. Pinch out the growing tips for a more bushy effect.

A number of varieties of *Scindapsus aureus* are used as house plants, each providing individual contributions to the degree and colouring of the variegations. *Scindapsus aureus* 'Golden Queen', for example, has yellow leaves with only spatterings of green; 'Marble Queen' has the same effect, except that in this case the leaves are mainly white. Neither of these varieties are easy to grow, however, and require more warmth and humidity than the standard species.

Scindapsus aureus is sometimes also known by the older Latin name *Pothos aureus*, hence its alternative common name, Golden Pothos.

Position: Bright indirect sunlight, especially for the more variegated forms, which need light to maintain their coloration.
Temperature: Standard room temperatures are fine, but they should not be allowed to drop below 50°F (10°C) in winter.
Water: Keep the soil moist in summer, but be careful of overwatering; in winter allow the soil to become quite dry before watering with tepid water. In hot, dry conditions, supply humidity by aerial-spraying, or by sponging over the leaves.

Feeding: Feed established plants once every other month in the summer.
Propagation: From stem cuttings or stem-tip cuttings; requires warmth and humidity.
Soil: Standard peat-based potting compost.
Problems: Brown spots on the leaves, leaves turn yellow: too much water. Falling leaves: not warm enough. Prone to common pests.

Sinningia speciosa hybrida
'Gloxinia'

The Gloxinia is usually only a summer guest to our homes, but a very welcome one, with its stunning display of large, bell-shaped flowers – red, purple, pink, white and bicolour, single and double – growing on short stems from a compact nest of low-lying foliage.

The Gloxinia is in fact a hybrid of the Brazilian *Sinningia speciosa*. The common name celebrates a French botanist of the eighteenth century, Benjamin Gloxin, and the Latin name refers to Wilhelm Sinning, the nineteenth-century German gardener who worked on the hybrids that were the ancestors of today's plants.

Although most people will discard their Gloxinias at the end of their summer flowering season (which can last up to two months), it is possible to keep the tubers from year to year. As the leaves die off, ease off the watering and then allow the tuber to dry off completely over the winter; start it off again in fresh, damp compost in early spring, giving it warmth (at least 70°F or 21°C) to begin with and gradually increasing the water.

The Gloxinia belongs to the same family as the African Violet, the Gesneriaceae. It has in common with this relative the fact that it needs to be watered rather carefully to prevent rot setting in: if you water from the base only, and do not allow the plant to stand in water, all should be well.

Position: Bright indirect light.

Temperature: Summer temperatures, when flowering, should be at least 60°F (16°C); avoid temperatures above 75°F (24°C). In winter, when the tuber is resting, any temperature above freezing is acceptable, provided that the tuber is quite dry.

Water: Supply plenty of water when in flower in summer, but water from the base. Humidity can be provided by standing the plant on a base of wet gravel; aerial-spraying is likely to damage the flowers and can result in rotting.

Feeding: Feed once a month when in flower.

Propagation: From seed, or by dividing the growing points by cutting up the tuber, or by pinning a leaf cutting to soil; all methods require warmth and humidity.

Soil: Standard peat-based compost.

Problems: Brown patches and signs of rot on leaves: too cold and wet. Prone to common pests, especially aphids.

Solanum capsicastrum

'Winter Cherry'

These bushes of small, deep-green leaves and copious, bauble-like fruits in green, yellow and orange make a delightful and timely decoration when they arrive in the shops around Christmas. As they ripen, the fruits grow larger and deepen in colour and can last for several months on the plant if kept in cool conditions. Perched all over the branches to the very tip, they look barely real, but real these fruits are, and not to be dismissed too lightly: they may look tasty, or may seem like tempting playthings to children, but they are in fact poisonous and can cause severe stomach upsets if consumed.

The Winter Cherry comes from Brazil and belongs to the

Solanaceae family, which also includes the tomato, the potato and the capsicums. The leaves and the tiny flowers that precede the fruit have a pungent odour, similar that of the potato plant.

The Winter Cherry is usually treated as a temporary visitor to our homes, to be discarded when the fruits have finished. New plants can be grown from seed in spring. Old plants can be kept a second year if you have the room to tolerate them during their rather less spectacular months (they can go in the garden after

Solanum capsicastrum

the last frost); if pruned hard in spring they are less likely to become straggly and should produce a fair amount of fruit.

A similar species is the *Solanum pseudocapsicum*, the Jerusalem Cherry. This has slightly larger fruits and smaller leaves, and is usually grown as a rather more robust bush than the *Solanum capsicastrum*.

Position: Plenty of light, including some direct light.

Temperature: When fruiting, cool temperatures are best, around 55°F (13°C). They will tolerate night temperatures as low as 40°F (4°C). Standard room temperatures are fine for the rest of the year.

Water: Water well and regularly when in fruit, and do not allow the soil to dry out. Keep the soil barely moist for the rest of the year. Supply humidity by daily aerial-spraying and place the pot on a base of wet gravel.

Feeding: Feed once a month when growing.

Propagation: From seed in early spring; requires warmth and humidity.

Soil: Standard loam-based potting compost.

Problems: Falling leaves: too much water. Flowers drop off without turning into fruit: poor light, or atmosphere too dry. Prone to common pests.

Syngonium podophyllum
'Goose-foot Plant' or 'Arrowhead Plant'

What sort of geese have feet like this? We have to allow a little poetic licence in this effort to describe the delightfully shaped leaves of this plant which, when young, are triangular with a deep incision on one side leading to the point at which the leaf is joined to its stalk. As the plant gets older, however, the leaves alter shape, branching out into more and more distinct leaflets until they become a star-shaped cluster of leaflets.

The leaves of this plant are its primary attraction: they have slightly crumpled surfaces which catch the light at different angles. The leaf-veins spread out from a central vein to meet a peripheral vein that lines the outer edge of the leaf. In the case of the pretty 'Emerald Green' variety, this outer vein is delineated by a sprinkling of light green, which is set off by the deep-green border. Another common variety, 'Albolineatum', on the other hand, has painterly splashes of white and light green cast freely over the otherwise deep-green leaves.

The Syngoniums are climbing plants that come originally from Central and South America; they are related to the Philodendron and require similar conditions. Like the Philodendron, they have aerial roots, if rather less developed; in a mature plant, these aerial roots will appreciate the moisture of a moss pole if you want the plant to climb. But this is also an effective trailer and looks good in a hanging basket, or in a stairwell. To keep the plant more bushy, and to prolong the life of the young, triangular leaves, pinch out the growing tips.

Sygonium podophyllum is sometimes also referred to as *Nephthytis podophyllum*. There is also another, similar species called *Syngonium vellozianum*.

Position: Bright indirect light, especially for the heavily variegated forms. The more green the leaves, the less light will be required.

Temperature: Warm conditions are preferred, 65°F (18°C) to 80°F (27°C). However, these plants will tolerate lower temperatures, provided they stay above 60°F (16°C).

Water: Water well in the summer when the plant is growing, but do not allow the pot to stand in water; ease off in winter, keeping the soil just damp. Humidity is important: spray with water daily in hot, dry conditions, and stand the pot on a base of wet gravel, or pack it in an outer container filled with damp peat, sand or moss.

Feeding: Feed established plants with a mild dose of plant food once a month when growing.

Propagation: From stem cuttings or stem-tip cuttings in spring; requires warmth and humidity.

Soil: Standard loam-based potting compost.

Problems: Yellowing leaves: too much water. Leaves wilt and fall: too cold. Prone to common pests.

Tillandsia ionantha
'Air Plant'

Air Plants are, more than most house plants, a matter of taste. The most common species look like some kind of diminutive form of tough, marshland grass and it is often hard to tell at a glance whether they are dead or alive. Certainly they do not do a great deal. But for all their lack of verve, Air Plants do have a certain fascination, partly because they make rather attractive plants in their modest way, and partly on account of the extraordinarily delicate mechanisms by which they cling on to life.

Air Plants form part of an informal group called the Grey Tillandsias, which in turn belongs to the Bromeliad family; like many of their relatives, such as the comparatively

Tillandsia ionantha

giant-sized Urn Plant (*Aechmea fasciata*), Air Plants are epiphytes – that is, in their natural habitat in South America they grow on other plants, usually trees, without actually feeding off them. Many Bromeliads use their roots only as a means of anchoring themselves to their hosts and gather their moisture and nutrients in the central vase-like rosette formed by the leaves. In the case of the Air Plants, they too use their roots only as anchors; for this reason they are often sold attached to pieces of cork-bark or shells, with no soil at all. As for moisture and nutrients, these they gather entirely from the air: on the wispy leaves there are tiny, silvery scales which take up the moisture in the air and convert it into all the plant needs for its survival.

The most common species of Air Plant is the *Tillandsia ionantha*, which has quite fleshy bases to its spindly leaves. It usually grows to about 3 in (75 mm) tall. The more grass-like *Tillandsia juncea* and *Tillandsia argentea* will grow to about twice this height. There is also the *Tillandsia caput-medusae*: this has the most peculiar, bulbous body crowned by curling tentacles, like an inverted octopus, or indeed, as the Latin name suggests, the head of Medusa – a plant that will appeal to anyone inclined towards the grotesque.

As with many of the Bromeliads, any of these Air Plants is capable of producing surprising flowers. The red and blue flower-head of *Tillandsia caput-medusae* is particularly beautiful. And like many of the Bromeliads also, Air Plants will fade away after flowering, but by this time should have developed young plants, or offsets, around their bases.

A relative of these Air Plants, and not to be confused with them, is the much larger *Tillandsia lindenii*, the Blue-flowered Torch, which has a spectacular cockscomb flower-head – a series of interleaved, pink bracts rising to about 1 ft (30 cm) high and producing blue flowers.

Position: Bright indirect sunlight.
Temperature: Standard room temperatures are fine, provided that they do not drop below 45°F (7°C).
Water: In a humid place, such as a bathroom or kitchen, watering may not be necessary; in drier conditions supply humidity by aerial-spraying, as often as once a day in the summer. Use lime-free water or rainwater for preference. No water need be supplied to the roots.
Feeding: Feed by mixing up a very mild dose of plant food with the water to be supplied by spraying, once a month during summer only.
Propagation: From offsets after flowering has finished.
Soil: No soil is required.
Problems: Dry tips to the leaves: air is too dry. Not flowering: needs more light, or feeding.

Tradescantia fluminensis
'Wandering Jew' or 'Inch Plant'

Wandering Jew, Wandering Sailor, Inch Plant or Spider-wort, this is one of the great favourites among house plants – easy to grow and interesting to watch as it develops. The genus is named after John Tradescant, who was gardener to Charles I; it comes originally from South America and still requires a certain amount of warmth to survive, but is strong enough to grow outside during the summer.

This is an ideal plant for the hanging basket, or for

trailing from shelves or mantelpieces. The basic variety has handsome, grass-green leaves growing on fleshy stems that are quite brittle and have to be treated with some care. The leaves grow all the way down the stems at regularly-spaced, jointed intervals, giving rise to the alternative common name Inch Plant. The variegated forms are particularly attractive, usually with green and cream stripes along the leaves, although some species (such as *Tradescantia albiflora* 'Albovittata') have silver-grey stripes. All these variegated forms are liable to revert to the original green, and a plant

Tradescantia fluminensis

that starts producing all-green leaves should have these removed completely the moment that they appear.

Another species is the *Tradescantia blossfeldiana*, which has similarly-shaped leaves, if a little larger, green and purple in colour, and covered in tiny hairs, giving them a velvet sheen, while the undersides are mauve.

Tradescantias are related to the Zebrinas, which are similar in many ways, although the leaves of the latter are slightly larger. *Zebrina pendula*, the Silvery Inch Plant, has a silvery sheen to the leaves. The variety of this called 'Quatricolor' has green, red, silver and pink leaves, but needs good light to maintain these colours. 'Purpusii' has purplish-green leaves with purple undersides, and no stripes.

All the Inch Plants will survive in fairly shady conditions, but they tend to become leggy and dull if starved of light. Pinch out the growing shoots if you want a more bushy plant. After some time in the house, a healthy plant may produce tiny white flowers: this gives you fair notice to take cuttings and to start fresh plants, as it is a sign that the mother plant has finished her span of years and will die as the flowers fade.

Position: Bright indirect light is best, although it will tolerate a fairly shady position.
Temperature: Standard room temperatures are fine, provided winter temperatures do not drop below 50°F (10°C). *Zebrina pendula* needs to be kept a little warmer than this.
Water: Water well whenever the soil dries out; use lime-free water for preference.
Feeding: Feed once a month from spring to early autumn, using a mild mix of plant food.
Propagation: From stem cuttings rooted in water, or placed directly in soil.
Soil: Standard loam-based compost.
Problems: Leaves become pale and dry out at the tips: too much sunlight. Plant becoming very leggy: not enough light.

Yucca elephantipes
'Spineless Yucca' or 'Yucca Plant'

The Yucca has become familiar to us in recent years, but no amount of exposure to this plant can quite dissolve the shock of its exuberant, arching leaves protruding from the top of a quite bare stem. These Yuccas are usually produced by forcing imported stems, or 'canes', to root and sprout in greenhouse conditions. This is why they do not grow from the very tip of the canes (as they would do if grown from seed), but to one side of the tip, giving the plants an even more unusual look. The fact is that Yuccas grow very slowly, so by producing what looks like a mature plant from a cane, the growers are able to supply a hungry market quickly with a product which, although still expensive, it is prepared to afford.

Yuccas come from South America: however, they are not

hothouse plants and are perfectly happy in a temperate climate. They actually prefer to be left to rest in cool conditions (around 45°F or 7°C) over winter. Yuccas can even stay outdoors for most of the year, and only need to be brought in when there is a danger of frost.

Yucca elephantipes

The *Yucca elephantipes* is the species most commonly available as a house plant; it is sometimes referred to as *Yucca guatemalensis*. Another kind of Yucca is also sold as a house plant, the *Yucca aloifolia*. Whereas the *Yucca elephantipes* may grow to about 1 ft (30 cm) across (the height will depend on the size of the cane), the *Yucca aloifolia* can have a span of some 3 ft (1 m). It is usually available as a young plant, and thus will grow on its own stem, producing a gnarled and rough-looking trunk as the old leaves fall away from the bottom of the rosette of foliage; by this means, growing at a rate of about 1 ft (25 cm) a year, it can sometimes reach a height of some 15 ft (4·5 m). It may also produce a spectacular fountain of creamy-white flowers after several years, but is unlikely to do so in the home. This is altogether a more noble plant than the *Yucca elephantipes*, but there is a drawback: its long, lance-like leaves are armed with needle-sharp points. It is only too easy to fail to see these and to receive a nasty poke in the eye: not for nothing is its common name Spanish Bayonet.

Position: Plenty of light, including direct sunlight.
Temperature: Standard room temperatures are fine; temperatures of around 45°F (7°C) in winter will allow the plant to rest.

Water: Supply plenty of water, especially during the summer.

Feeding: Feed with a mild dose of plant food once a month during the summer.

Propagation: From offsets in spring, or from cane sections taken from an old plant (requires warmth and humidity).

Soil: Standard loam-based potting compost.

Problems: Yellowing leaves: poor light, or waterlogging. Prone to common pests, especially scale.

Cacti

Cacti are so much a world of their own among house plants that they deserve a separate section, however brief. For one thing their classification is not simple, so it is not really possible to lump them all in under one Latin name along with all the other house plants in the A–Z.

In any case, cacti *are* different. What distinguishes them from other plants, however, is not immediately obvious, and the range of plants included under the title is extremely diverse. Botanists have divided cacti into three families: the Pereskieae, which usually have woody stems and fleshy leaves; the Opuntieae, which are made up of a chain of segments dotted with tufts of bristles called 'glochids', as, for example, the Prickly Pear; and the Cerei, most of which (but not all) have a single, tubular stem and spines. What all these groups have in common is areoles – tiny bumps on the surface of the plant, sometimes marked by a tuft of woolly hair or bristles, from which the spines, new growth and flowers will develop.

Cacti form an important group within the much larger informal group known as succulents. Succulents have thick, fleshy stems in which they can store water: among the succulents it is only the cacti that have areoles.

Almost all cacti come from North and South America: only one genus, *Rhipsalis*, has been found growing naturally outside the Americas. From the point of view of house plants, cacti can be most conveniently divided into two groups, each of which requires slightly different treatment: desert cacti and forest cacti. The vast majority of these come from the Cerei family.

Where water is scarce, all forms of life have to find the means to preserve moisture. In the case of the desert cacti, the solution is threefold: to store water in their thick stems; to prevent the loss of moisture through having tough, waxy skins; and, by being armed by an array of vicious spines, to ward off thirsty predators which would dearly like to get at all the accumulated moisture stored in the stems.

It would be wrong to think that it never rains in the desert: from time to time there will be a deluge, followed perhaps by years of drought. Desert cacti have a root-system to deal with this: shallow but very extensive, to mop up as much water as possible before it evaporates or drains away. It would be wrong also to think that it is always boiling hot in the desert. Because there are few

Chamaecereus silvestrii

clouds in arid regions, there is no cloud-cover to keep in the heat when the sun has gone down: night temperatures in inland deserts can be decidedly chilly, as too can the winters. Some cacti, furthermore, only grow in cold areas, such as the mountainous desert of the southern Andes, which is perpetually cooled by the ocean currents sweeping in from Antarctica. Cacti do not, therefore, need high temperatures all the time, and indeed most are happier and more likely to flower if they spend the winter at cool temperatures.

And flowering is something that is definitely to be encouraged. Flowers play an essential role in the reproduction of plants, which are often dependent on insect life to carry out the necessary cross-fertilization. In a tough environment, competition is tough: the plants producing the most spectacular or most enticingly fragrant flowers stand the greatest chance of attracting the insects vital to their reproduction. So it is that cacti produce some of nature's most extraordinary, most lavish and vivid flowers, and will do so in the home as well, given the right conditions.

Most of the rotund, spiny plants that the word cactus conjures up are desert cacti. A typical one is the *Echinocactus grusonii*, the Golden Barrel, a ball of spines growing on a concertina-like body. The concertina effect provides an ingenious method of expanding to contain more moisture when it is available, and contracting in times of drought as the moisture is used up. The *Stenocereus* or *Cereus thurberi* uses a similar stratagem, and although as a house plant it remains a manageable size, in the wild it becomes the towering thicket 20 ft (6 m) tall that is familiar to us in Western movies and goes by the apt common name of Organ-pipe Cactus. Others include the *Ferocactus*, or Barrel Cactus, with its pink or red curved spines and orange or yellow flowers; *Cephalocereus senilis*, the Old Man Cactus, so named for the long white hairs that grow from its single, tubular stem; *Chamaecereus silvestrii*, called the Peanut Cactus on account of its tumble-down pile of short, stubby stems that look like unshelled monkey-nuts, and which can produce an array of bright red, multi-petalled flowers that last for up to a month in the early summer; the *Mammillaria bocasana*, the Pincushion Cactus, with its hooked spines and white hairs and pretty little yellow flowers, striped in pink; and many, many more, each with its own pleasures and peculiarities, and each with its own merciless form of defence which makes careful handling absolutely essential. (Use thick gloves when doing anything like repotting: the spines are hard to remove once embedded in your skin and can cause infection.)

Forest cacti come from a rather different world, with different demands. Most of these are epiphytes, living in the branches of trees, and storing water in their succulent stems which, in the rather less aggressive environment of the treetops, are generally not coated with spines. The most common and popular house plant among these is the *Zygocactus truncatus* (also called *Schlumbergera truncata* or *Epiphyllum truncatum*), the Christmas Cactus or Crab Cactus. This produces trailing branches made up of a series of small, nearly triangular segments, which do precious little for most of the year. Come Christmas-time, however, it produces beautiful blooms from the tips of the stems: white, pink, red or purple. That is, it will if it is feeling good-natured, which it will not do if you move the plant when in bud, and if it is not kept in comparatively cool conditions.

Zygocactus truncatus

The Christmas Cactus today is usually a hybrid, and often grafted on to another cactus base. This is true of other forest cacti as well, such as those of the *Epiphyllum* genus which are grown for their impressive flowers, such as the *Epiphyllum* hybrid 'Paul de Longpré', with its bright yellow blooms that can grow to some 6 in (15 cm) wide.

Forest cacti include the only non-American genus, the *Rhipsalis*, among which is the *Rhipsalidopsis gaertneri* or *Schlumbergera gaertneri*, the Easter Cactus, similar in many ways to the Christmas Cactus except, of course, for the season in which it chooses to flower.

Position: Desert cacti like to be in the sunniest position possible, summer and winter; forest cacti like bright indirect light.

Temperature: For most cacti average temperatures in the summer are fine; in winter they should be kept cooler, but not below 40°F (4°C), and some, such as *Cephalocereus senilis* need 60°F (16°C) in winter. Flowering forest cacti should be kept in cool winter temperatures of 55–60°F (13–16°C).

Water: Cacti should be watered well and then the soil should be allowed to dry out. The best method is to sink the pot into a basin of tepid water until bubbles cease to rise up from the soil; then drain well. Desert cacti should be kept barely moist in winter. Bring water to budding or flowering forest cacti, as they must not be moved. It is mainly only the forest cacti that like humid air, which can be supplied by aerial-spraying.

Feeding: Feed once a month during the summer, or when flowering.

Propagation: Usually from cuttings and offsets, or seeds germinated in warmth and humidity.

Soil: Standard loam-based potting compost, with a third volume of added sharp sand.

Problems: Overwatering, especially in cold weather can cause rot; lack of water can cause wilting. Prone to common pests, especially mealy bug, red spider mite and scale.

Index